Murder in the Rainforest
The Yanomami, the Gold Miners and the Amazon
Jan Rocha

LAB

**LATIN
AMERICA
BUREAU**

survival
of tribal peoples

30 years

© 1999 Jan Rocha   All rights reserved.
First published in 1999

In the U.K.:
Latin America Bureau (Research and Action) Ltd,
1 Amwell Street, London EC1R 1UL
The Latin America Bureau is an independent research and publishing
organization. It works to broaden public understanding of issues of human
rights and social and economic justice in Latin America and the Caribbean.

A CIP catalogue record for this book is available from the British Library

ISBN: 1 899365 37 0

Editing: Jean McNeil and Ralph Smith
Cover photographs: Jerry Callow/Survival International (top) and Carlo
Zacquini
Cover design: Andy Dark
Printed and bound: Russell Press, Nottingham

PREFACE – A NOTE

The inhabitants of Haximú were until recently a very isolated group of Yanomami. With the arrival of the gold miners in their lands they became the victims of a situation of total cultural and social misunderstanding.

The importance of this book is to remember the genocide committed at Haximú against the Yanomami. To forget it means to permit it to happen again.

Claudia Andujar
Photographer and CCPY coordinator
São Paulo, Brazil

I remember Haximú and the Yanomami who lost their lives. I can't forget this and I am talking to you so that you can help us and tell it all in the book, telling other people who never saw or heard about the Haximú massacre. We Yanomami never thought that the whites would kill us, but they killed 18 Yanomami and we saw it. We saw that they are very dangerous and like to kill Indians like animals; they think we are animals but on the contrary, it's animals that kill people. We also will never forget the families who died. Their children are there thinking that we don't want what happened in Haximú to happen ever again. I don't want the *garimpeiros* to go there and kill again and I don't want our blood to flow again.

Davi Kopenawa

AUTHOR'S NOTE

Murder in the Rainforest is the story of a massacre that shocked the world when it happened, although it had been waiting to happen for some time. This book is also an indictment of Brazilian government policy towards one of the last large groups of indigenous peoples who still live in a traditional way, the Yanomami.

Nineteen gold miners were tried for genocide because of the events described in this book. Two are serving prison sentences, but the others have never been caught. The politicians and businessmen who financed, supplied, and profited from their activities have not had to answer for their actions. Nor have the presidents, ministers, governors and congressmen who betrayed their constitutional duty to protect the Yanomami and their environment. Nor have the military officers who chose to forget the army's own historic example of respect and tolerance for indigenous people been called to account.

At the same time this book is a recognition of those individuals in the federal police, in the public prosecutors' office and in FUNAI who did their best to elucidate the events at Haximú and bring those guilty to justice.

Jan Rocha, London

CONTENTS

The diagram shows the route the survivors took to escape, going from Haximú to Marcos to Toototobi

AUTHOR'S ACKNOWLEDGMENTS

The idea for writing this book came from Claudia Andujar, who has dedicated her life to the cause of the Yanomami ever since she first became aware of their plight. She also gave me invaluable assistance in writing it.

Much of the book is based on the writings and first-hand accounts of two anthropologists, Bruce Albert and Alcida Ramos, who have both lived and worked with the Yanomami for many years. It also draws heavily on the writings of geographer Gordon MacMillan, who spent several years in the Amazon basin studying the goldmining process.

Invaluable information was also provided by attorney Aurelio Rios of the Public Prosecutor's Office, journalist Eliana Lucena of FUNAI, and Carlo Zacquini, who has spent years with the Yanomami and is coordinator of the CCPY's (Pro-Yanomami Commission) work in Boa Vista. Many other members of the CCPY team in both São Paulo and Boa Vista have provided information and encouragement. My thanks to all of them, and also to Fiona Watson of Survival International who has given vital support, encouragement and information, at every stage of the book.

I would especially like to thank Davi Kopenawa, who, on behalf of the Yanomami, has given his help and blessing to this attempt to tell the real story of Haximú and what it has meant to the Yanomami.

Finally I should like to thank FAFO of Norway and Oxfam for believing in the project and providing the funds for getting it written and produced, and to the staff of Latin America Bureau in London for their attentive editing of the manuscript.

All royalties for this book will go to CCPY.

Jan Rocha

1
CHRONICLE OF A MASSACRE

Garimpeiro Amigo!

15th June 1993: six Yanomami youths are on the way back to Haximú, their village, deep in the Amazon rainforest. The trail follows the Orinoco river. They stop to eat the cassava flour they were given by some *garimpeiros*, or gold miners, at the last miners' camp they visited. The expedition has been only partly successful, because the miners have not given them a rifle they want. As they eat, they hear a crashing and snapping of twigs. It's the sound made by white men hurrying through the forest – Indians move through the forest silently.

Seven *garimpeiros* appear – Goiano Doido, Caporal, Careca, Goiano Cabeludo, Parana Aloprado, Luiz Rocha and Uricado Branco – the same ones who were playing dominoes when the Yanomami visited their hut to ask for food. They want the Indians to go hunting tapir with them. The Indians feel there is something strange about this sudden invitation, but the gold miners are armed, while they have only one rifle between them, so they agree. They fall into line along the narrow trail, 18 year-old Reikim leading the way, followed by the others, alternately gold miner and Indian. They walk on, until Paulo Yanomami, who is carrying the Indians' only rifle, stops, hands it to Bauxi and disappears into the forest to defecate, telling the others to go on, because he will catch up with them.

But the gold miners do not go on. Instead one of them seizes the arm of Bauxi, who is now holding the rifle, and fires his sawn-off shotgun at point blank range, hitting him in the abdomen. The other miners turn their guns on the remaining four youths. One of the Indians crouches down, his hands over his face, pleading in the few words of Portuguese he knows, '*Garimpeiro amigo!*' (gold miner friend). Careca shoots him in the face and he falls dead on the path. Makuama and Kaperiano are also shot dead, and then three of the gold miners aim their guns at Reikim, taking it in turns to fire at him. He plunges into the trees, twisting and turning in a desperate attempt to escape the bullets. The first two miss; the third hits him. But by now he is hidden by the thick forest, and, reaching the bank of the Orinoco river, he plunges into it and submerges, just coming up to breathe.

Treading water, dazed and bleeding, he watches the riverbank. He sees the gold miners hastily bury three bodies, and search for the fourth victim, who, although fatally wounded, has managed to crawl away, probably falling into the river further along and being carried away by the current. One of the miners comes right down to the edge of the river in the search and sees Reikim hiding in the water. He scrambles back up to get his gun and finish him off, but realizing he has been seen, the youth swims further down river. Meanwhile Paulo Yanomami, from the bushes, has heard the shooting and dives into the river to escape. He swims as fast as he can, eventually coming ashore near Haximú. In the village he tells the others about the ambush. There is consternation.

Two days later, in spite of the danger, Paulo returns with a group of men and women to the scene of the killing to look for the bodies. As they approach it they find the wounded Reikim who has been hiding in the bushes. He tells them the place where the bodies are buried and describes what happened.

For the Yanomami, the gold miners have committed not one, but two terrible crimes. They have not only killed, but they have buried the bodies of their victims. The Yanomami always cremate their dead. The Indians search unsuccessfully for the body of the fourth youth, then dig up the three bodies, carry them deeper into the forest and light a funeral pyre for each. After the cremations, the charred bones are put in baskets and taken back to the village for the funeral rites. Fifteen to twenty days later, the funeral ceremony is held. After a ritual hunt, the bones are pulverized and the ashes are placed in calabashes and sealed with beeswax. Three friendly villages are invited for the ceremony, Homoxi, Makayu and Toumahi.

Then it is time for revenge. In accordance with Yanomami tradition, violent deaths must be avenged by menfolk. If the killers cannot be found, then other men must be killed – never women and children. A group of kinsmen sets out from Haximú, covered in black *genipapo* dye and carrying bows and arrows, machetes and their only rifle.

Revenge

After two days' walk the warriors near the mining camp and camp out for the night, their presence undetected. At ten o'clock the next morning, in the rain, they creep near the open-air kitchen where two men, Neguinho and Fininho – many *garimpeiros* are known only by their nicknames or first names – are cooking beans over a fire. An Indian called Macuxi steals behind a tree and shoots. Fininho is hit in the head and killed instantly. Neguinho, although

2

hit in the back, escapes into the bush, while three other gold miners, hearing the shots, flee. The warriors then attack the dead miner, shooting arrows into the body, splitting the head open with blows from an axe. Before escaping back into the forest, they seize everything they can find in the hut, including bullets and the dead man's rifle.

This revenge is not enough for all of the Indians; while the rest of the people in the village are preparing to go to a feast at the nearby village of Makayu, three young warriors set out for a new attack. The leader is the brother of the dead youth whose body is still missing. Unable to perform the appropriate funeral rites, the brother has a special desire for revenge. The three reach a mining site. The deafening noise of the pumps covers the sound of their movements. They are close to a miner before he perceives their presence and throws his arm up, stopping the bullet aimed at his head. The three Indians escape and make their way back.

Fearing more attacks, the entire village of 85 people has moved out of their two communal huts and camped out at an abandoned cassava field, between Haximú and Makayu, where they believe they will be safe. There they wait for a formal invitation from the Indians in Makayu to the feast.

The messengers arrive. The Haximú Indians must go to the feast, but because of the miners' attack and their own counter-attacks, the community is on a war footing. They decide to send only adults without children to the feast, so they can get there and back quickly. The old people and the women with children are left behind. As women and children are never targets for Yanomami revenge attacks, there are no fears for their safety.

After the adults have left, the three young warriors who have attacked the gold miners arrive back. They have been travelling through the forest, avoiding the regular trails. This is why they fail to spot the heavily armed group of gold miners now on its way to seek revenge for the killing of Fininho.

Attack

When *garimpeiros* throughout the region learn of the death of Fininho, they are furious. The dead man is buried where he died, and the wounded Neguinho, found hiding in the forest, is carried for two days in a hammock to the Raimundo Nene airstrip, to be put on a plane and flown out for treatment. The gold miners decide that they will put an end to the Indian nuisance once and for all. They will kill everyone in the two communal huts at Haximú. The planning of the counter-attack begins.

3

Men are recruited from different mining camps; weapons and ten boxes of ammunition are collected. The four principal mining bosses in the region offer their support for the operation. To reinforce the *garimpeiros'* firepower and ensure success, two of them, João Neto and his brother-in-law Chico Ceará, hire gunmen and supply weapons and ammunition. Meetings are held to plan the attack. The other two leaders are Eliezer and Pedro Prancheta, who had written the note which provoked the first killings. The note read 'Let these suckers have it', and it was given to the six young Yanomami by the men at the first hut they visited, to pass on to the miners at the second hut. The Yanomami, who could not read Portuguese, had no idea what was written in the note, much less that it would be interpreted as a death sentence.

On 21 July, the revenge party sets out, determined to kill all the Indians at Haximú. The fifteen men are heavily armed. Between them they carry fifteen rifles, seven .38 revolvers, machetes and knives. After a trek of two days they reach the first Haximú communal house, but find it empty. They move on to the second house, but it is also empty. As it is getting dark they spend the night in the second hut, and the next morning start looking for the Indians. They discover the path that leads to the abandoned cassava field, and the makeshift shelters where the Yanomami are camping.

Massacre

23 July: early in the morning, most of the women leave to collect *ingá* fruit some distance away, taking with them many of the children. About nineteen remain in the camp, including the three young warriors. It is after 10 am when the group of gold miners reach the camp. They see children playing, women cutting firewood, an old blind woman sitting, a baby lying in a hammock. One man opens fire and the others follow, shooting at anyone, man, woman or child. Paulo Yanomami, surprised in his hammock, hears shots and sees a gold miner reloading to fire at him. Running for his life, he plunges into the thick vegetation that surrounds the huts. A handful of others, including several wounded children, also manage to escape and hide near him.

After shooting everybody they can see, the attackers search the huts, stabbing with their knives everyone they find there, injured and uninjured. Finally, in their vengeful fury, they mutilate the bullet-ridden bodies. Goiano Doido does not spare even a small baby lying in a hammock, wrapping it in a cloth and cutting it to pieces with a machete. The old blind woman is kicked to death.

4

When they have finished twelve Indians are dead: three old people – one man and two women; a young woman called Masena, visiting from Homoxi; three adolescent girls; three boys aged six to eight; a three year-old girl and a one year-old baby girl. The ground is soaked with blood. Among the terrified children who have escaped into the bushes is a ten year-old girl with a serious head wound from which she will later die, and two small girls of six and seven, wounded with leadshot in the face, neck and arms.

The survivors listen as the shots and screams gradually die out. They hear the goldminers saying 'let's go, let's go'. When they are sure the goldminers have gone, they creep out of their hiding places and back to the scene of slaughter. Among the bodies, Paulo Yanomami finds that of his three year-old daughter.

Sated with killing, the gold miners return via the village of Haximú and set fire to the two communal huts. They pile up all the cooking pots and utensils they can find and discharge their guns and rifles at them. Mission accomplished, they make their way back to the mining camp.

For nearly a month, nothing happens. The *garimpeiros* resume their mining operations, now undisturbed by Indians. Apparently the massacre has gone undetected. Then one night, listening to the news on Radio Nacional, they discover that the killing of a large group of Yanomami Indians has become national news and has provoked national and international indignation and outrage.

Panicking, they decide to leave the area immediately, and begin the two days' march to the clandestine Raimundo Nene landing strip, where the planes that supply the mining camps operate. There they force their way on to the first planes to appear, threatening to kill anyone who informs on them, saying 'we'll do the same we did to the Indians'. Among those recognized at Raimundo Nene are Pedro Prancheta, João Neto, Pedão, Chico Ceará and Goiano Doido. From Boa Vista, most of them disperse to different parts of the Amazon, some perhaps to neighbouring countries. Meanwhile, equally panic-stricken, the survivors of the massacre have hastily cremated their dead and fled the scene, terrified that the *garimpeiros* will return to finish them off.

5

2

'THE YANOMAMI ARE WEEPING'

Like a slow-burning fuse, news of the massacre travelled from the depths of the forest, gathering speed until it exploded in Brasília, the Brazilian capital. On 17 August, 24 days after the attack on Haximú, the Boa Vista coordinator of the Brazilian government's Indian affairs department, FUNAI, received a handwritten letter from Sister Alessia, a French nun working for the government health service at the Yanomami village of Xidéia. It said:

> The Indians from Yababak are all here. The *tuxaua* [chief], Antonio, says they do not want to go back because the *garimpeiros* went to a *maloca* nearby and killed seven children, five women and two men, and destroyed the *maloca*. A few men managed to escape. I believe it is true because they are terrified. I asked the FUNAI people here to send a radio message asking the Federal Police to investigate the case. They said that first they needed to be sure. They went to an airstrip near here to see if there were *garimpeiros* there, but what happened was at a *maloca* on the border with Venezuela by name of Haximú, we don't know how many people live there. We just have news of it from Indians here who visit there. It's a *maloca* which has little contact with Mapi. I ask you to see what you can do. Talk to FUNAI there so we can discover the truth.
>
> Thank you,
>
> Sister Alessia

The next day, 18 August, Sister Alessia's letter was sent to FUNAI's headquarters in Brasília, and to its president, Claudio Romero, marked 'for your information'. Romero acted quickly: he requested a Brazilian Air Force helicopter to take a team to the scene of the alleged massacre, tentatively identified as somewhere between the villages of Homoxi and Xidéia.

In Brasília the Ministry of Justice, to which FUNAI is subordinated, lies just across the road from Congress. The same afternoon the Minister, Mauricio Correa, was due to make a statement about changes in indigenous legislation to one of the permanent congressional committees, so he had invited Romero to go with him. As they crossed the road and walked down the slope towards the futuristic building that houses the Congress, Romero mentioned the news that had arrived earlier. He said that up to 70 Indians might have died.

Xidéa 12-08-93

Prezado Luis

Recebi cópia da carta do deputado amigo seu, acredito que vai dar certo muito agradeço por isto, aproveito desta carta para dizer o que esta acontecendo aqui que nos preocupa, os índios de yolabate estão todos aqui e Tx Antonio dizendo que não querem voltar porque os garimpeiros foram em uma maloca próxima a deles um dia de caminhada e matou sete crianças cinco mulheres dois homens e destruir a maloca, poucos homens conseguiram fugir acredito ser verdade pois estão amedrontados. Pedi na funai aqui para passar um radio pedindo para a policia federal investigar o caso disseram que primeiro precisam da certeza, foram em uma pista proxima daqui ver se la tem garimpeiros, mas o que aconteceu e em uma maloca diversa com venezuela morre Haximu nos não temos o censo dela temos noticia por indios daqui que vão la e uma maloca de pouco contato com map. Peço ver o que pode fazer falar com funai ai para que possamos saber a verdade, obrigado.
Ir Alessia

Sister Alessia's letter

Bombshell

In August 1993 not much was happening in Brazil. The main story was the national soccer team's progress in the preliminary rounds of the World Cup (which they went on to win). So when, at the end of his statement on indigenous policy, the Minister asked the deputies to be quick with their questions because he was concerned about the news he had just received of a massacre, and was in a hurry to find out more about it, the bored journalists lethargically covering the session came suddenly to life. The Minister mentioned the numbers he had been given by Romero: maybe 60 or 70 dead. Within minutes phones were ringing in the newsrooms of every newspaper,

7

radio and TV network in Brasília, Rio and São Paulo, and the Indian massacre became the lead story on every bulletin.

The next morning, 19 August, the front page of every major Brazilian newspaper carried the story. The *Folha de S.Paulo* headline screamed 'At least 19 cut to pieces by *garimpeiros*'. The next day the same paper's headline read: 'Forty die in Yanomami massacre: FUNAI expedition finds mutilated and cremated bodies'. For the next week the Yanomami dominated the news. The numbers escalated, there were denials and accusations and diplomatic incidents. Politicians, policemen, military chiefs and anthropologists brandished theories about the motives, causes and consequences of the massacre. Some tried to deny it had ever taken place, calling it a farce. The world's press took up the story. Reporters poured into Roraima looking for bodies.

The survivors, meanwhile, completely unaware of what was happening in the outside world and still terrified of the vengeful fury of the *garimpeiros*, continued their headlong flight through the forest.

Later in the day on 19 August the first direct news of the massacre arrived in Brasília in a radio message sent by FUNAI official Wilk Celio. Accompanied by federal police agents he had flown over the area in a helicopter and seen two communal houses 'totally destroyed by fire'. After landing they found domestic utensils peppered with bullet-holes and slashed with knives. The message read: 'human skeletons in an advanced state of decomposition were found stop indians said that bodies had been carried by relatives to the Simão *maloca* for the cremation ceremony stop from the description of the survivors we estimate that there were at least 30 people in the village.'

The same day news of the massacre was already on its way, straight from the heart of Yanomami territory, to the UN in New York. An American linguist, Gale Gomez, had been working in the village of Demini with French anthropologist Bruce Albert on a CCPY project to prepare a bilingual health manual for the Yanomami. Already the Yanomami in Demini suspected that something terrible had happened. On August 8th a group of Indians from another village had camped near Demini and in the exchange of news had passed on a story about five or six Yanomami men being murdered near the headwaters of the Orinoco.

Demini leader Davi Kopenawa took the news seriously and sent a radio message to FUNAI in Boa Vista. Then on 19th August, Davi picked up a message on a two-way radio saying that up to 19 Yanomami had been killed by gold miners. He immediately wrote a communique which Gomez translated into English. The handwritten note was then sent via a passenger on the next

CANADA'S NATIONAL NEWSPAPER

THE GLOBE AND MAIL

150TH YEAR

WEEKEND EDITION

No. 44,838

Toronto, Saturday, August 28, 1993

A tragic, confusing tale of genocide in a remote Brazilian rain forest has shocked the world.

COVER STORY

Was there a massacre in the Amazon?

DIÁRIO DE RORAIMA

Massacre na reserva Ianomami
19 índios são mortos em conflito com garimpeiros

PF não contém
contrabando
de ouro em RR

Miners 'behead' children during Amazon attack

With a Yanomami leader, Justice Minister Maurício Corrêa inspects ruins

BRAZIL

Rain-Forest Genocide
Mystery surrounds the massacre of the Yanomami, hindering efforts to track down their killers

By MICHAEL S. SERRILL

The Times 20.8

9

plane to Boa Vista, where the English version was faxed from CCPY's office to the UN in New York with instructions to pass it on immediately to the UN office for Human Rights.

After the unexpected level of media attention, the Minister of Justice, Mauricio Corrêa, consulted FUNAI president Claudio Romero about going in person to the scene of the massacre to find out what had happened. Romero now had confirmation of the story, and told the Minister 'it is even worse than we thought'. He suggested the killings might have been a reprisal against FUNAI for its operations to remove the *garimpeiros* from the Yanomami area. Corrêa invited the Attorney General, Aristides Junqueira, to go with him to the Amazon.

But FUNAI press officer Eliana Lucena was worried about the dimensions the story was now taking on. The press wanted proof of the massacre. Brazil's influential weekly news magazine, *Veja* (which a year earlier, during the United Nations Conference on Environment and Development (UNCED) Summit in Rio, had trumpeted under a cover picture of him with the headline 'SAVAGE!' an unconfirmed story accusing the Kayapó leader, Paiakan, of rape) was sending a photographer up to Roraima, and he wanted bodies. Eliana, who had had twenty years' experience covering Indian affairs for a Brazilian national newspaper, knew that the Yanomami cremated the bodies of their dead.

Mystery

Later the same day the Minister, the Attorney General and the FUNAI president left their air-conditioned offices in Brasília, boarded a Brazilian Air Force jet and flew 2,000 miles to the north of the Amazon rainforest.

When they landed in Boa Vista, they were met in the air force hangar by Comandante Bournier, Commander of the Jungle Infantry Battalion. He told them: 'We don't know what's happened, or indeed, if anything has happened.' A federal attorney who had flown up with the party recalls: 'it was extremely disagreeable because we still didn't know what had really happened, and there was Bournier saying nothing had happened. Bournier then advised them not to go to the area, but Aristides Junqueira said it would be absurd to fly all the way up there and not go to the Yanomami area.'

A new problem then arose: a group of Roraima officials and politicians had gone to the airfield to greet the illustrious visitors and they now insisted on accompanying the party into the Yanomami area. Romero, the FUNAI president, who did not like these local dignitaries, tried to stop them with a bureaucratic argument, saying they did not have permission to enter an

10

indigenous area. The leader of the local legislative assembly, who was standing in for the governor, replied that, as interim governor, he did not need permission. As the highest authority present, the Justice Minister should have sorted the problem out, but he was feeling unwell and remained inside the plane.

It was left to the Attorney General to smooth the ruffled feathers and include the local legislators in the party, which then transferred to a piston-engined Bandeirante aircraft for the trip to the army base at Surucucus, inside the Yanomami area, not far from the Venezuelan border. There they met the FUNAI team who had made the first trip to the burned remains of the village. By now night had fallen, so they slept at the base. The air force pilots plotted the coordinates for the location of the village and concluded that it was inside Brazilian territory. On 20 August the Minister flew to the village of Homoxi by helicopter.

By now the press were arriving and the tiny airfield in the middle of the forest was crowded with small planes. (Romero, while trying to keep out local politicians, had given *carte blanche* to the press, saying 'FUNAI should not under any hypothesis cover up any type of information involving the revolting episode or spare any effort to discover the responsibility of the murderers and their bosses.') Reporters whose normal beat was the political jungle of Brasília suddenly found themselves in the rainforest, hot and sweaty, still dressed in their city clothes. As the Minister climbed out of the helicopter he was startled to find himself surrounded by seven Yanomami warriors in black war-paint, chanting war-cries and shaking bows, arrows and clubs at him. One of them was Davi Kopenawa, one of the very few Yanomami who speaks Portuguese, and the only one to have travelled widely outside their territory. He explained they were preparing for war against the *garimpeiros*, not against the Minister.

FUNAI workers had managed to make a clearing in the forest big enough for a helicopter to land only six minutes walk from Haximú, the village which had been attacked. It was another 20 minute helicopter ride from Homoxi. The Minister and his entourage flew up there on the final leg of their trip from the certainties of the capital to the mystery of the forest. TV crews filmed the Minister examining the bullet-ridden cooking pots, animal bones and ashes. Something terrible had happened – but where were the bodies? Only one skeleton could be seen – where were the others?

Back at Homoxi, FUNAI *sertanista* (field worker) Francisco Bezerra had been talking to Antonio, a Yanomami who was at the feast in the village of Makayu when the distraught women from Haximú appeared with their terrible

11

story. Antonio was an inhabitant of Homoxi, but Bezerra's inadequate command of the Yanomami language led him to a disastrous misunderstanding. He believed he had found a survivor from Haximú, overlooking the unlikelihood that any of the real survivors would have stayed near the place of the slaughter instead of fleeing. And when Antonio gave the names of all the men who lived in Haximú, and counted up their wives and children on his fingers, Bezerra concluded that Antonio was listing those killed: 73. The 'survivor' was introduced to the Minister, who solemnly questioned him through the interpreter. The news flashed around the world: 73 Yanomami – 35 adults, 35 children, and three still in their mothers' wombs – had been killed. The Attorney-General began to talk about genocide.

But in Boa Vista everyone was busy denying the massacre. The state governor, Brigadier Ottomar Pinto said it was all an 'invention' by those who wanted to get the demarcation of indigenous lands speeded up. He said, 'Up till now they haven't found a profusion of bodies'. Airton Cascavel, president of Roraima's legislative assembly, accused FUNAI of inventing it. *Garimpeiro* leader Altino Machado dismissed it as 'just a fight between Indians', although he was aware that one of the men who took part in the killings had escaped aboard one of his planes. Federal police delegate Sidney Lemos said: 'Up until now there is no material proof of the massacre – FUNAI spoke of 30 to 40 dead but we don't have a single body.' In view of Lemos's obvious lack of interest in elucidating the case, Junqueira decided to appoint a special federal police investigator, Raimundo Cotrim.

On 22 August, two days after the Minister's visit, a federal police team went back to Haximú. This time they found the ashes of the eight cremation fires lit by the survivors before they fled. In their report they described the 'macabre findings': spent bullets, human hair and teeth among the ashes of the fires. They also found a vital clue to the identity of the murderers: scores of imprints of football boots, the favoured footwear of Brazilian *garimpeiros*.

Terrified that they too would become the victims of *garimpeiro* attacks, 60 Yanomami arrived at Xidéia from nearby villages, seeking shelter. Davi Kopenawa said they had warned FUNAI a month before about the return of the *garimpeiros* but nothing had been done. 'Whites [authorities] only come to the area when people die.' In an open letter he asked for the definitive removal of all the *garimpeiros* who were still working in Yanomami land:

> The criminals must be caught, tried and put in prison. Not just them.
> The businessmen and politicians who are responsible for these
> *garimpeiros*, who send them to fight with the Yanomami should also be
> tried. All the Yanomami are very worried about this massacre because

the same can happen at Catrimani, at Demini, at Toototobi and other distant places where there are no FUNAI posts or FNS [government health] posts or missions.

These are the words of my anger at what has happened.

Yanomami leaders from all over the area gathered at Homoxi and mourned the dead. They held a mourning ritual after seeing the evidence of the massacre – ashes and bones – but decided not to take part in the search for the *garimpeiros*, because 'arrows don't have the strength of guns'.

The Minister flew back to Brasília. To his embarrassment, the press had discovered that Haximú was in fact not in Brazilian territory, but, according to the maps of this remote area, inside Venezuela. To the Yanomami such national borders were meaningless, but in international diplomacy it was a considerable *faux pas*. Unwittingly, the Brazilians had invaded the neighbouring country's airspace, cleared a helicopter landing site and carried off the remains of a Venezuelan village for forensic examination.

VENEZUELA

Venezuela has a slightly larger Yanomami population than Brazil, with an estimated 12,500 living between the Orinoco and Branco rivers. In 1911 the Venezuelan government delegated to the Roman Catholic missionaries of the Salesian order authority over all the Indians in the territory of Amazonas, including the Yanomami. 'At the beginning extremely conservative and paternalistic in their relationships with the Indians, severely criticized by local anthropologists ... in the last few years the missions have profoundly modified their form of working with the Yanomami in the light of the Second Vatican Council and the Medellín Conference (1968)', wrote Marcus Colchester.

In 1979 the creation of a Biosphere reserve was first proposed to protect the Yanomami, whose land rights, like those of other indigenous groups, were not recognized by the Venezuelan state. Pressures from the north of the country to 'develop' the region came and went according to the fortunes of the oil industry, Venezuela's main source of revenue.

In 1989, Brazilian gold miners began crossing the border to escape the police operation launched to remove them from the Yanomami reserve in Brazil. The idea of a reserve to protect the area was revived. In 1991, the Upper Orinoco–Casiquiare Biosphere Reserve, covering 83,000 sq. km, was created with European Community financing of US$8 million, for the 'protection and development of Yanomami society and the conservation of

---

13

the region's rich natural resources'. The aim was to involve the indigenous population in the administration.

The territory of Amazonas became a state in 1992, with Puerto Ayacucho its capital. The state's new legislative assembly then divided it into six municipalities, splitting up ethnic groups and forcing others to coexist with their ancestral enemies. The new law also allowed common lands to become the property of municipal administrations. Indigenous communities, who have no property deeds to their traditional lands, could then have been evicted and the land sold to mining companies or ranchers. According to the CCPY's (Pro-Yanomami Commission) Update 92, the new law contravened the constitution, which defines Venezuela as a multiethnic and pluricultural state which respects cultures, traditions and collective land tenure of the indigenous peoples, with a ban on mining activity until the year 2050.

The Supreme Court of Venezuela overthrew this law in 1997, recognizing the right of the indigenous peoples of the state of Amazonas to participate in its territorial division. Three hundred delegates from nineteen ethnic groups met and drew up their own plan, proposing seven areas, including a special separate area for the Yanomami. Instead of mayors these new 'municipalities' would have a form of collective government run by co-ordinators.

Over the years the Venezuelan government has launched various development programmes for its Amazon region – for example, CODESUR, PRODESSUR – for the sustainable development of the south. The common denominator of these plans is that they were drawn up in centralized ministries in Caracas, with minimal local participation, and do not survive the change of administration at each presidential election.

In April 1997 president Rafael Caldera signed bilateral agreements with President Cardoso for the paving of the Brazil–Venezuela highway and the supply of hydroeletric energy from Venezuela's Guri dam. Both these projects went ahead, but another proposed project, to link the Amazon and Orinoco rivers by dredging the Casiquiare canal to make it navigable for large ships so far remains on the drawing-board.

Repercussions

In the days following the news of the massacre international response grew, with protests outside Brazilian embassies and consulates in Washington, New York, Houston, San Francisco, London and other European capitals, and at the United Nations organized by Survival International. Letters from anthropologists and other international organizations begin to pour in.

Under pressure to act, President Itamar Franco called an emergency meeting of the National Defence Council, made up of ministers and top military leaders. The council, presided over by the president himself, decided that a special federal police unit should be set up at the Surucucus army base to investigate exactly what happened, and that the installation of a planned US$1.2 billion radar system, SIVAM, to cover the entire Amazon region, should be speeded up.

The most unexpected decision was the creation of a new special Ministry for the Amazon, headed by the Brazilian ambassador in Washington, Rubens Ricupero, an experienced diplomat who had helped negotiate a co-operation treaty in 1977 between the countries who shared the Amazon. It was called 'the Extraordinary Ministry for Articulated Actions in the Legal Amazon'. (Later it became the Ministry for the Environment as well, and in 1995, when the Yanomami massacre had dropped completely out of the news, 'Amazon' was replaced with 'Hydraulic Resources'). In Congress a parliamentary committee of inquiry was set up to investigate the massacre.

While the outside world investigated their fate, in the other world of the forest the Haximú survivors were still intent on flight. The ten year-old girl had died from her head wound, and been cremated by her distraught parents. The other two injured girls were carried on their parents' backs. But now at last they were nearing friendly territory, where they hoped to find rest and refuge.

In Brasília, questions about possible ulterior motives for the killings began to be aired. The *Folha de S.Paulo*'s usually well-informed political gossip columnist, Painel, wondered whether the government's real concern was to discover 'who is behind a tragedy of this sort in the Amazon, knowing that there are those who are interested in turning it into an international territory?' A retired air force brigadier, Ivan Moçyr da Frota, reflecting the opinion of the influential nationalist lobby amongst the military, questioned whether the massacre had really happened, saying 'Powerful countries may have paid the Indians to say there was a massacre.' He suggested that they had filmed abandoned villages to transmit to the world a distorted idea of how the Indians are treated, 'although no country treats its Indians as well as Brazil.' The brigadier said that a crime demands bodies, murder weapons and motives, and none had been found.

Ottomar Pinto, the Roraima governor, also insisted on the 'invention' theory. He said it has been invented by those who wished to speed up the demarcation of Indian lands, like the 'progressive clergy' and foreign

15

companies interested in getting their hands on the minerals in the reserves. For the Attorney General, who believed that a massacre had taken place, the opposite was true: economic interests opposed demarcation precisely in order to get their hands on the minerals.

But the appeal to nationalist sentiment and raising of the bogey of foreign interests was enough to cause problems for two diplomats from the US and Canadian embassies in Brazil, who had obtained FUNAI permission to visit the scene of the massacre and arrived at the Surucucus base on 23 August. They were stopped on orders from the Brazilian Foreign Office and not allowed to go any further. A *New York Times* editorial headlined 'Death in the Tropical Forest' added fuel to the nationalists' fire. The Army Minister found his own scapegoat. The size of the Yanomami reserve was to blame for the violence: '94,000 hectares is much too big an area for a few Indians.' For the Minister, the *garimpeiros* were also victims.

The Yanomami are Weeping

As confusion about what had happened grew, Yanomami leader Davi Kopenawa, who was helping in the search for clues in the Haximú area, insisted that proof of the massacre had been found:

> We found many fires, charcoal, with lots of bones. Many little bits, because the heat of the fire destroys, breaks up the bones. Many people could have been incinerated. We found many bones pounded into ashes. We make a wrapping out of banana leaves. We put everything in it and pound it, and then put it in a gourd. These bundles were found at the camp. In the forest we found calibre 12 bullet-cases, and holes from a revolver and from leadshot. There is already much that proves they killed many of our relatives.

Kopenawa explained why the Yanomami cremated their dead: 'The ashes are for the family to remember, to remind them. They are kept ten months, a year, up to two years. Every year or two years, feasts are held until the ashes are all gone. Not all at once. A little bit at a time'.

He said the *garimpeiros* invaded the Yanomami reserve because they have not got jobs or land:

> As they don't have anything, they are angry and they want to come into our reserve. They are pushed by others, who are behind them. They attack the Yanomami and have people to defend them in the city. They have lawyers, journalists, and enough money to avoid being arrested. *Garimpeiros* are never arrested and they continue doing this.

The guilty ones are those who stay in the city, living in good houses, without dirtying their hands, without using any energy. The *garimpeiros* are being paid to kill Indians, to create problems, that's why they are dangerous. The *garimpeiros* are always smiling. The Yanomami are weeping. Later the *garimpeiros* will pay for our death. They will pay dear. Their children will suffer. They will pay because their families will suffer eating rubbish in the streets, thrown into the streets. This is happening with children because of their parents' mistakes, and the mistakes of the government and the politicians.

3
INVESTIGATION AND TRIAL

Many *garimpeiros* were angry about the massacre; some because they did not agree with the killing of women and children, others because it had brought them as a group into disrepute, and forced them to abandon their prospecting in the forest.

Meanwhile, José Altino Machado, their self-styled leader, had fallen out with João Neto, already suspected of being one of the leaders of the crime. The special federal police investigator who had replaced Sidney Lemos, Raimundo Soares Cotrim, traded on these divided loyalties to find *garimpeiros* who were prepared to tell what they knew. He also set about locating the women employed in the mining camps as cooks – sometimes, though not always, a euphemism for prostitutes. Cotrim soon had a list of suspects.

By 21 August he felt confident enough to ask for an arrest warrant for João Neto. Neto, whose real name was João Pereira de Morais, had been active inside the Yanomami area for four years, searching out good gold areas, setting up mining camps, organizing planes to transport *garimpeiros* and machinery, but he himself lived in considerably more comfort in the capital. The federal police began searching for him in the bars, nightclubs and other places in Boa Vista frequented by *garimpeiros*. But João Neto had disappeared, abandoning his home and his business. Most of the others on the list had also vanished.

The few who were eventually located and brought in for identity parades looked completely different: in the *garimpo* they went unshaven, wearing tattered, mud-spattered shorts. To the Indians, they all looked alike. In the city they were cleanshaven, and they wore shirts and trousers. In the eyes of the Indians, they had changed out of all recognition. But the cooks recognized them.

The Survivors

On 24 August, as controversy still raged about whether or not a massacre had taken place, and how many had died, a radio message arrived at the office of the Commission for the Creation of a Yanomami Park (CCPY) in Boa Vista. It was from the CCPY doctor, Claudio Esteves de Oliveira, at the Balawaú health centre, deep in Yanomami territory. He said that Yanomami returning from a hunting expedition told of meeting a group of wounded

Indians, who said they had survived an attack by *garimpeiros*. They were heading for the post at Toototobi. The doctor asked for a plane to be sent to Toototobi and then set out with other members of the CCPY medical team, Jorge Gurgão and Manoel de Souza, to find the survivors. They found them in the Marcos *maloca*, near Toototobi: an exhausted, traumatized group, carrying two small girls with bullet wounds and 14 gourds containing human ashes.

Providentially, French anthropologist Bruce Albert, one of only a handful of outsiders to speak the Yanomami language, was also at the Balawaú post, advising on a CCPY health project, as was Davi Kopenawa. They flew immediately to Toototobi. As Albert and Davi listened to the horrific details still fresh in the minds of the survivors, the real story of what had happened at Haximú finally became known. The next day, 26 August, Bruce Albert's handwritten report reached the CCPY office in Boa Vista. It provided definitive evidence of the massacre, and was published in the *Folha de S.Paulo*.

Albert wrote that on 25 August, 69 survivors from Haximú arrived at the Marcos *maloca*, among them three with bullet wounds, a man aged about 20 and two girls aged about six and seven. The women's faces were covered in black crusts, formed by dust and smoke mixed with the tears they had rubbed into their faces during funeral laments. 'During a long meeting with several of the survivors we managed to reconstruct the circumstances and events leading up to the Haximú massacre.' He noted that the 'pseudo-survivors' interviewed up to then by the press and FUNAI were in reality inhabitants of Homoxi who had been at the feast at Makayu and were only indirect witnesses.

After questioning the survivors Albert concluded that 13 Indians had been killed: one old man, two old women, one middle-aged woman, three young girls, four small boys aged between six and nine, and two baby girls aged three and one. Three were injured, one of whom died later. He also established an exact date: the survivors said it had happened when the previous moon was beginning to wax, which meant 22 or 23 July. The Indians told Albert how and where they had cremated the bodies, leaving only the body of Masena, the visitor from Homoxi. Albert noted that only bits of this body had been found by the federal police and the Yanomami:

The Indians from Demini had found a trail made by white men leading from the *tapiri* [temporary shelter] where the killings took place to the Haximú river, a tributary of the Orinoco, and bloodstains on the riverbank in a recently cleared space. All this seems to indicate that the *garimpeiros* returned, cut the body into pieces and threw it into the river. During this return to wipe out evidence they must have burned down the *malocas*, throwing the tools left at the *tapiri* in the river.

After many hours of listening and questioning, Kopenawa and Albert were able to reconstruct exactly what had happened, where it had happened, who had died, who had killed them, and what had happened to the bodies. The Indians also gave the names of those *garimpeiros* they had identified. The mystery was solved.

The Investigation

Most of the *garimpeiros* had disappeared, but Cotrim, the special federal police investigator, used the evidence of the cooks to piece together the story from the other side. On 6 September he took a statement from Eva Souza who had cooked for João Neto from June to August. She said she had heard that Goiano Doido had killed three or four Indians. She herself had gone to see the bodies of the three young Indian men killed in the first incident. She gave the names of the group who had set out to kill the Indians, and she had been there when they returned. 'One of them had cut open a baby with a knife'. Another cook, Silvania Santos Menezes, aged 19, who also worked for João Neto, was afraid to talk at first because she had received threats. She said she also went to see the bodies. She had heard that one Indian knelt down and said *'garimpeiro amigo'*, and that Careca had shot him in the face. She confirmed that the Indians had been promised hammocks and clothes by João Neto. Altogether Cotrim collected the names of 23 suspects.

On 6 September he located Juvenal Silva, a *garimpeiro* from the Taboca area who denied being involved in the massacre but said he knew about it. On 7 September Cotrim found and detained Pedro Emiliano Garcia, one of the four for whom an arrest warrant had been issued. Garcia decided to talk. He denied taking part but said he knew who did it. He admitted sending the note 'Let these suckers have it' to Eliezer. He gave a physical description of 17 men. He told Cotrim that Pedão was a notorious hired gun from Mato Grosso, and gave a list of all the murders attributed to him and Parazinho, another gunman. Later, before the judge, Garcia retracted his confession.

On 9 September Judge Renato Martins Prates ordered 19 of those accused of taking part in one or both of the killing episodes to be detained for 30 days for investigations. He also asked for their real identities, as all those involved were known only by their nicknames. Only two, Pedro Prancheta (Pedro Emiliano Garcia) and Eliezer (Eliezo Monteiro Negri), were found and arrested to await trial. During the police investigation 38 people – *garimpeiros*, cooks, Indians, and others – were heard.

On 15 September a request was made to Venezuela to authorize the entry of a police helicopter for further investigations. Brazil had not apologized to Venezuela for the inadvertent invasion of its territory by the Minister of Justice, but as it had been established beyond any doubt that the massacre had taken place on Venezuelan soil, the Brazilian authorities now depended on the good offices of their counterparts there to continue the investigations *in loco*. No one had any doubt that the perpetrators were Brazilian, which meant that although they had killed in Venezuela, they could be prosecuted in Brazil.

A few days before the massacre the Public Prosecutors' offices of both countries had signed a memorandum of understanding providing for the exchange of information. Now they decided on a joint investigation, beginning with an exchange of relevant documents. But for reasons best known to itself, the Brazilian Foreign Office insisted that all exchanges should take place through diplomatic channels, according to the rules of the Vienna Convention. It then refused to allow Brazilian documents to be passed to the Venezuelans unless documents were also received, and failed to press for the exhumation of the body of the *garimpeiro* who had been killed. The collaboration which the Brazilian public prosecutors had counted on to help elucidate the massacre ceased before it had begun. Instead, each country pursued separate investigations.

The Venezuelan inquiry was conducted by a judge in Puerto Ayacucho, in the state of Amazonas, where the Haximú village was located. The inquiry was hampered from the start by the Venezuelan government's reluctance to supply the logistical support needed to carry out investigations. Only on 29 September was a government plane made available to take the judge to Haximú, 40 days after the Brazilians had been there and carried off all the evidence, including the remains of the uncremated Indian woman. The Venezuelans never requested the return of these objects. At Haximú the judge examined the by now much-trampled scene of the crime, found a few burnt bits of bone and some spent bullets, and interviewed some Yanomami Indians who knew about the events. Further requests for a plane to fly the judge to Toototobi to interview the survivors were ignored by Venezuela's Foreign and Defence Ministries and the inquiry ground to a halt.

Although the Indians were considered Venezuelan citizens, the government made no effort to ask for the extradition of the *garimpeiros* who had killed them. In Caracas, congressman Rafael Elino Martinez accused the government of being co-responsible for the Yanomami massacre. Venezuela's Foreign Minister, Fernando Ochoa Antich, admitted that the Amazon frontiers were unprotected because government funds were going instead on bureaucracy and paying the foreign debt. As a result, even after the massacre Brazilian *garimpeiros* continued to operate freely inside Venezuela, including at least some of those accused of the massacre, who were later sighted across the border.

On 15 October the team of federal prosecutors presented formal accusations against nine *garimpeiros*. Led by experienced attorney Luciano Maria Maia, Carlos Frederico Santos and Franklin Rodrigues da Costa had devoted weeks to poring over the evidence and studying Yanomami culture.

On 29 December 1993 the appeals of the only two being held were allowed, and they were released from custody into house arrest. The prosecutors appealed against the judge's decision.

Time passed. Four hearings had to be postponed because the federal police claimed that they could not locate five cooks and two *garimpeiros* called as witnesses. The police said that with only nineteen agents in Roraima it was impossible for them to find those wanted as witnesses. On 23 March 1994 FUNAI sent a plane to bring two of the survivors, Waythereoma and Paulo Yanomami, to Boa Vista to give evidence. Not surprisingly, Paulo was unable to recognize Pedro Prancheta, who was present at the hearing. These were the only two Yanomami witnesses heard by the judge.

José Altino Machado, the *garimpo* leader and businessman, was called. He claimed that a pilot called Pé Na Cova (Foot in the Grave) had come to him and asked him to spread the story that the massacre was really no more than a brawl between Indians, but when he discovered that children had been killed he refused. According to José Altino, the attack was not premeditated, otherwise they would have taken more ammunition and not 'been forced to use their knives.' They thought that in such a remote community, with people of such little value, it would never be discovered.' Altino also claimed that the Haximú Indians had been moved into the area by Venezuelan police (National Guard) and were not the original inhabitants. He said the Venezuelan police trained Indians to attack *garimpeiros*.

The Evidence
Bruce Albert discovered that the Haximú survivors had with them 14 gourds containing the ashes of their murdered kin. The gourds were kept in baskets

Survivors holding the
ashes of relatives killed

Carlo Zacquini

or wrapped in cloths. In the eyes of Brazilian law, which demands material proof of murder, this was the only evidence that the massacre had taken place. But for the Yanomami the ashes were sacred, and must be used in the funeral rites. 'The ritual treatment of the bones of the dead is the central, indispensable point of funeral ceremony', says Albert. First the bones are cremated and pulverized and placed in a gourd. Later they will be used in large-scale inter-community rites, and then buried near the fires of their families. The ashes of children will be mixed with banana pap and eaten.

The prosecutors faced a dilemma: should they try and examine the ashes, violating the Indians' cultural code, or respect the code but run the risk of prejudicing the investigations? They debated what to do. Murder demanded proof. The vociferous anti-indigenous lobby in Roraima continued to deny that a massacre had taken place. Even the national newspaper *Folha de S.Paulo*, after covering the news of the massacre in depth, gave two pages to a previously unknown intellectual to defend the theory that it was all a farce. On the other hand, the constitution assured indigenous peoples the right to their own social organization, customs, language, beliefs and traditions. This meant they had the right to give their dead the treatment demanded by their traditions. They had already had to abbreviate the funeral rites, cremating the bodies hurriedly, instead of allowing them to decompose on a platform in the forest.

In the end the prosecutors opted for a compromise. Bruce Albert identified the ashes in each of the gourds by name, and each was photographed being held by a relative. A woman called Manakaima held a gourd with the ashes of her one year-old granddaughter. The widow of Elisio held the gourd with the ashes of her husband, an old man. A young man called Simão, who had been wounded in the attack, carried the gourd containing the ashes of an adopted son, aged six or seven, and the gourd of another relative. Reikim, the young man wounded in the first attack near the river, carried the ashes of the young girl who had been promised as his wife.

But one body had remained uncremated, the body of the young woman visitor, Masena. In life Masena, whose age was put at between 18 and 22 years old, had never gone beyond the boundaries of the neighbouring villages. In death she was flown to the forensic department of the Federal Police in Brasília. The police report states 'On 27 August 1993 we received for examination a cardboard box containing a skeleton, fragments of burned bone, hanks of hair and a wrapping of banana leaves containing a viscous substance similar to black earth.' The pathologists reported finding bullet holes in the skull and knife wounds to the arms, abdomen, chest, head and legs, as well as a deep cut on the right-hand side of the face, which had opened up her head. Leadshot was found encrusted in her spinal cord. The experts concluded that shots had been fired first at a distance of five to ten metres, hitting her in the chest when she was standing, and then at close range (less than two metres) at her head, when she had fallen down, weakened by the probable huge blood loss.

After the autopsy, Masena's skeleton was returned to her relatives for ritual burning in spite of the protests of scientists who wanted to keep it for further study. In their statements the Yanomami referred to Masena as a living person, because she had not been cremated. In the remains of the funeral fires the police had also found 118 fragments of carbonized bone, two semi-burnt teeth and human hairs. When these ashes were returned to the survivors they were accompanied by a warning not to eat them, because they had been treated with chemicals. The injured survivors, who had been examined by Dr Claudio Esteves de Oliveira, still had leadshot embedded in their bodies. Simão Yanomami found it difficult to chew because of the shot

24

in his jaw. The police experts concluded that their wounds were compatible with the weapons known to have been used by the *garimpeiros*.

Genocide

The prosecutors decided that the *garimpeiros'* actions against the Haximú Indians amounted to genocide, the intentional destruction of a human, racial, religious or national group. Brazil has been a signatory to the UN Convention on Genocide since 1952. In 1956 Congress passed a law specifying the punishments for those found guilty of genocide, defined by Professor Heleno Fragoso, a leading Brazilian criminal lawyer, as 'actions that are not primarily directed against the life of an individual, but rather against groups of people, in their totality'. The prosecutors reasoned that the Indians had been attacked not as individuals but simply because they were Indians.

The *garimpeiros* wanted revenge for the attacks by Indians on them. They killed Indians whose names they did not know, against whom individually they had no reason for hostility. Their hostility was impersonal. They 'challenged the Yanomami's right to existence'. They intended to wipe out the whole village. Only the coincidental invitation to the feast at Makayu and the early morning expedition to pick fruit had prevented a much greater number of Yanomami from being killed.

The Trial

After the success of the initial investigations, it seemed that there was enough evidence to make a good case against 23 *garimpeiros*, but only two of them, Pedro Emiliano Garcia and Eliezio Monteiro Neri were detained, and then for only a short period. When Cotrim was transferred from Boa Vista the federal police did little to pursue the investigations or arrest the other accused.

As often happens in Brazil, the legal system proceded slowly. Months dragged by. On 16 May 1995 the public prosecutor sent a letter to the federal judge in charge of the case in Boa Vista, asking him to inquire of the federal police what had been done to identify, locate and arrest the other 21 accused and to find and hear witnesses. The *garimpeiros'* lawyers claimed the Indians were not original inhabitants of the area, but had been moved there by the Venezuelan National Guard and armed and trained to attack the *garimpeiros*. In support of their claim that the attack had not been premeditated, the defence said the *garimpeiros* 'had been forced to use their knives' because their ammunition ran out. The four young men, according to the defence, had died during a shootout.

In early December 1996 the US-based Center for Justice and International Law (CEJIL), Human Rights Watch and several Venezuelan human rights organizations denounced the Brazilian government to the Organization of American States's (OAS) Inter-American Commission on Human Rights in Washington as responsible for the massacre of the Yanomami through negligence and omission. In their petition they said: 'The Brazilian government should be held responsible for not having effectively prevented the presence of *garimpeiros* in Yanomami territory, which led to innumerable, often violent conflicts with the Indians...' They also accused the Brazilian government of showing a 'lack of diligence' in bringing to trial and punishing those responsible for the massacre.

It was not until 19 December 1996, three and-a-half years after the murders had been committed, that federal judge Itagiba Catta Preta Neto sentenced Pedro Emiliano Garcia (Pedro Prancheta) João Pereira de Morais (João Neto) Elezio Monteiro Neri (Eliezer) Francisco Alves Rodrigues (Chico Ceará) and Juvenal Silva (Curupuru) to a total of 98 years and six months' imprisonment for the crime of genocide. Each received a sentence of nineteen years and six months, except Pedro Prancheta, who got twenty years and six months. The judge said they had committed the crime in particularly cruel circumstances, against defenceless women and children, and that the genocidal act had caused the migration of an entire indigenous community. They were motivated by feelings of revenge for the attacks they had suffered.

For the judge the fact that the crime had been committed in the morning, by surprise, against Indians who were in their natural habitat was an aggravating circumstance. He acquitted them of the other charges that had been brought against them: hiding the bodies, forming a criminal gang, smuggling and illegal mining. When the judge handed down his sentence, none of the accused was in detention. However, later that same day federal police arrested João Neto in Boa Vista and he was taken to the prison there to begin serving his 20-year sentence. Pedro Emiliano Garcia (Pedro Prancheta) had been sighted at a jungle airstrip near Parafuri, in the Parima mountain range in January 1996. He was finally detained in August 1997. The others have been variously reported to be in mining camps inside the Yanomami area and in Venezuela. Two of the 23 originally accused, Maranhão and Parazinho, who were said to have killed the Yanomami children, were later reported to have been killed themselves – Parazinho shot dead by other *garimpeiros* in another Amazon mining camp, Maranhão in Colombia, where he had fled. These deaths have never been confirmed.

26

Meanwhile, as the trial dragged on in Boa Vista, the 69 survivors of Haximú were trying to come to terms with life in a new place. They had chosen the village of Marcos in the upper Toototobi region in Brazil as their refuge, because it is a long way from the *garimpo*, the CCPY health teams make regular visits, and they had relatives who had been living there since the previous year. In their minds, all these things made it a safe and desirable place to live, and they intended to start planting manioc as soon as the rainy season ended, in September or October.

Even so, when Dr Marcos Pellegrini visited the survivors a year later, he found them in a state of depression. They had built a new community house, but they did not live in it because they said it was occupied by the ashes of the dead. Their sickness and death rates were higher than those of the host community. Haximú survivors accounted for twelve out of fifteen cases of malaria and five out of seven deaths in the Toototobi region. The doctor reported that they asked many questions about the aftermath of the massacre: 'They asked if the police had beaten the *garimpeiros* who killed their relatives, and why the white chiefs still sent *garimpeiros* to their land. They said they were fearful, because they were still being hunted. They demonstrated a profound sadness, especially because they had never found the bones of one of the dead' (the young man who fell into the river after the first killings).

During a row between the survivors and the other Indians one day, Dr Pellegrini heard the oldest surviving Haximú woman shout out that the whites had killed her brothers, her husband, her children and even her domestic animals. She said they still wanted to kill and send diseases, that her life was bad and her thoughts were 'poisoned', that she did not want to continue living like this.

Could the massacre have been prevented?

The trial of the perpetrators of the Haximú massacre focused on the guilt of a handful of individuals. Yet the massacre at Haximú did not take place in a vacuum. There had been many warnings that something terrible could happen. In July a Brazilian reporter called Carlos Wagner arrived in Roraima to write a special series, for his paper *Zero Hora*, on the gold miners. *Zero Hora* is published in the southern state of Rio Grande do Sul, and Wagner had never been to Roraima before, but it did not take him long to discover what the *garimpeiros* were up to. In his article, published on 27 July 1993, he wrote:

There is a conspiracy under way in Roraima. The *garimpeiros* expelled by the Federal Police are preparing a new invasion for September when the level of the rivers goes down. At the moment 500 of them are hiding in the forests of the Yanomami area. One of the mining bosses, Roberto Fernandes da Silva, forecasts that there will be 15,000 of them by the end of the year. They used green clothing so as not to stand out among the trees, worked manually to avoid the noise of machinery, and camouflaged their airstrips to escape detection from the air. The pilots and the planes expelled when the Yanomami area was closed off by the federal police have begun to return. 'We are back in the fight again', said one of them.

The *garimpo* planes are parked at clandestine airfields on ranches around the capital. 'We know they are back,' said Sidney Lemos, federal police delegate.

Wagner interviewed Elton Rohnelt, whose mining interests, as owner of the GoldAmazon company, had not prevented him being chosen as Environment Secretary by the governor of Roraima. 'There's no development without conflict', said Rohnelt. 'Our deputies in Brasília have told us that the government is not going to release any more money for removing clandestine miners from the Yanomami area', said a gold trader. 'We can't let the gold miners go hungry when there is so much gold waiting to be found.' The price of gold had risen on the New York stock exchange by over 23 per cent between January and August 1993.

4
THE YANOMAMI WORLD

The Yanomami mostly inhabit the densely forested watershed between the Orinoco and Amazon basins. The frontier between Venezuela and Brazil runs through their traditional territory. They number about 22,500, making them the biggest indigenous group in the Americas who still live largely according to traditional hunter-gatherer ways.

Invasion of their lands began on a large-scale in the 1970s with road-building and continued in the late 1980s when the Amazon goldrush took off. Previous contact had been limited to Catholic and Protestant missionaries and sporadic, sometimes violent, contact with rubber-tappers, Brazil nut collectors and hunters after animal pelts.

In 1989 the anthropologist Alcida Ramos, who had spent many years with the Yanomami, was asked by the Attorney General's office to give expert evidence in support of the Yanomami case for the demarcation of their lands and the expulsion of the invading gold miners. She wrote:

> Originally the Yanomami lived in the Parima mountains. Over the centuries they have dispersed widely, reaching the lowland river valleys both to the south, in Brazil, and to the north, in Venezuela. Today their territory extends over an area of more than 9 million hectares in Brazil and nearly 10 million in Venezuela.

> Whenever possible, the Yanomami choose village sites on high ground, away from large rivers. The water supply comes from small streams or springs usually located some distance from the houses. There is a considerable variation in temperature between mountain and plains villages. In the region of the Parima–Pacaraima range, altitude may reach 1,000 metres above sea level, which results in chilly nights and pleasantly warm days with temperatures reaching 30 degrees Celsius.

> There are essentially two well-defined seasons: the dry season lasts from December to May and the rainy season from June to November. But even during the dry season it usually rains at least once a week in sparse, quick showers. In the rainy season the landscape is drastically transformed; small streams with crystal-clear beds turn into vast muddy

Carrying food baskets past gardens of manioc   *Fiona Watson/Survival International*

torrents; little cosy groves in the forest where people camp in dry months become amazing tangles of vegetation which one has to cut through on gathering trips for frogs, miniature fish, crabs, vines while other forest areas become flooded areas impossible to cross on foot. Lagoons seem to appear as if overnight, driving away animals and most people. In turn, the dry season is a time of plenty; game animals such as paca and capybara are easy prey when the streams are low and the animals have to come closer to the river banks, to the fields and even to the villages. It is the time for visits, for collective hunts, for family camping in the forest, and for the ceremonies in memory of the dead.

As a result of the seasonal variation, natural resources vary throughout the year, and the Yanomami are experts in exploiting these climatic and ecological differences: they know every detail of animal behaviour, about plants and the weather. As a whole they prefer small streams to big rivers, as their size fits more comfortably the scale of family activities that are part of their traditional way of life; the streams' edges, very often muddy, display footprints of game animals, crab holes, traces of enemies, and a whole host of signals they easily detect. Along these small streams, the Indians have inscribed a geography that is also history. These waterways are, as it were, the veins and capillaries that irrigate not only with water but also with memory and cultural meaning the practical and symbolic body of the communities. Along their courses, news flows from village to village as people run after fish they have stunned with the *timbó* vine in the dry season.

Just as important are the trails that connect various villages. More direct than the streams, they trace routes that are permeated with memories and tales that the Yanomami recall on their short or long trips through the forest in search of raw materials and food or when visiting other villages. They recount stories of memorable hunting trips, of encounters with spirits, or of enemies caught in hiding. Radiating from each village, these trails compose an elaborate network of paths that link the village to new and old fields, to hunting grounds, to gathering and fishing sites, to summer camps, and to neighbouring as well as distant villages.

For Alcida Ramos these trails are like 'conveyor belts carrying the social impulses that keep alive the great chain of relationships between communities and render isolation and atomization of the local groups virtually impossible. They are, in other words, like nerves constantly transmitting the flow of social meaning that underlies villages, gardens, the forest and the relationship between humans and spirits, that is, the supernatural.' Trails and streams make up a vast network that links all of the approximately 300 communities in both Brazil and Venezuela, over an area of about 19 million hectares.

The Yanomami have developed their social system over a long time. The first reference to them by white explorers was made in the eighteenth century, but linguistic studies indicate a history of at least 700 years. As they cremate the dead, and the hot, humid weather destroys rather than preserves houses and artefacts, there is almost no raw material for archaeologists to work on. But for Ramos, 'the way in which the Yanomami exploit their natural resources is the result of a long tradition passed on through countless generations and has attained a point of equilibrium in spite of extremely poor soils, so that they have succeeded in sustaining a growing population without depleting the forest'. She concludes:

It is unquestionable that the Yanomami in Brazil need a territory of over nine million hectares; not only to maintain an economic, social and political standard of living that has proved its efficiency in the preservation of the rainforest for centuries, but also to guarantee the necessary space for future generations to provide continuity to their culture. All of these considerations show very clearly not only that the Yanomami are capable of extracting a sustainable livelihood from their environment, but that it is they who can adequately protect the ecological stability of their territory. Experience acquired through the course of many generations has enabled them to deal imaginatively and rationally with the delicate balance of their habitat.

Besides hunting, fishing and gathering, each Yanomami family has a garden, cleared from the forest by slash-and-burn methods, where they plant manioc, bananas and tubers. Because of the soil's low fertility, a garden remains productive only for two to three years, so a family will have more than one on the go, each at a different stage: an old one, now overgrown with weeds but still yielding fruit, another in full bloom, a third defined but yet to be planted. The forest quickly regenerates itself once the garden is abandoned. Ramos explains:

> The forest, of which the gardens are small interruptions, is the basis for the territorial circumscription of a village or group of villages. This is what the Yanomami call *urihi*, home, the place where one belongs.' The forest may shelter spirits, but it also provides game and practically all the raw materials needed in the village: 'poles and leaves for house building, fibres and vines for hammocks, ropes, basketry and fishing weapons, for transportation and baby slings, resins for torches, wax for sealants, and an infinity of other products.

To maintain this self-sufficiency, the Yanomami need a large area. When game becomes scarce in one area, they move and build a new village. One geographer calculated that a group of 84 people required a minimum area of 640 square kms to provide everything they needed for production and reproduction. This seems a lot to those who live in cities, but in the Amazon region, where population density is extremely low, it is perfectly possible. In Brazil the 10,000 or so Yanomami live in 150 villages of between 25 and 140 people.

The villages consist of one large, or two or three smaller, round communal huts, or *malocas*. The largest *malocas* can be as high as a three-storey building.

Yanomami children by a river   *Jerry Callow/Survival International*

Openings in the outside wall are closed at night. Inside there is usually a wide open-air arena, used for dancing and ceremonies. During the day children play there. All round the edge of the arena, protected by the roof, each family has its own space where they make their fire. Around here they hang their hammocks and possessions, and at night each family space is marked by the flicker of flames from a fire.

The Yanomami need to constantly hunt and forage, and theirs is normally a healthy diet. Game and fish provide plenty of protein, while in the forest they find nuts, fruit and honey, and the garden supplies fruit and root vegetables. The Yanomami take from the forest only what they need; they clear no more than the space required to grow food.

Like other indigenous peoples, they have evolved land use strategies over the centuries, which are so well adapted to local eco-systems that they are often indistinguishable from nature. They know about forest management because they have been practising it for hundreds of years. The result is that although they have lived in this area since time immemorial, the forest was intact until the roadbuilders and the *garimpeiros* came. Having plenty of space also enables them to solve feuds between rival factions by allowing dissident groups to split off and build a new village. In this way new groups are created

Boys in front of a
traditional *maloca*

*Jerry Callow/
Survival International*

every two or three generations and the problem of too many people competing for the same resources is avoided. Good relations with neighbouring villages are maintained by invitations to feasts that can last several days, at which gifts are exchanged.

Outsiders have found the Yanomami to be essentially a peaceful, good-humoured people, although feuding between different groups occurs. Before firearms were introduced by the *garimpeiros*, fights would involve clubs and end in injuries, rarely in death. The sensationalist theory propounded by US anthropologist Napoleon Chagnon that the Yanomami are a bloodthirsty, 'fierce' people who regularly kill each other is not supported by other anthropologists or anyone who has lived with the Yanomami for years.

34

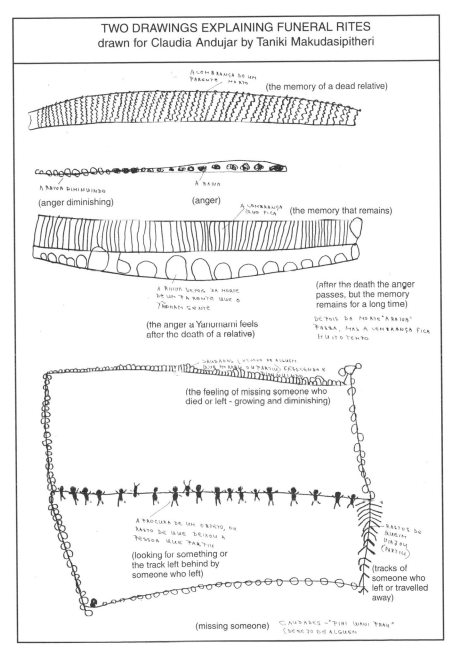

TWO DRAWINGS EXPLAINING FUNERAL RITES
drawn for Claudia Andujar by Taniki Makudasipitheri

A LEMBRANÇA DE UM PARENTE MORTO (the memory of a dead relative)

A RAIVA DIMINUINDO
(anger diminishing)

A RAIVA
(anger)

A LEMBRANÇA (QUE FICA) (the memory that remains)

A RAIVA DEPOIS DA MORTE DE UM PARENTE (QUE O YANOHAM SENTE)

(the anger a Yanomami feels after the death of a relative)

(after the death the anger passes, but the memory remains for a long time)

DEPOIS DA MORTE "A RAIVA" PASSA, MAS A LEMBRANÇA FICA HUITO TEMPO

SAUDADES (DESEJO DE ALGUEM QUE HORRERU OU PARTIU) CRESCENDO E DIMINUINDO

(the feeling of missing someone who died or left - growing and diminishing)

A PROCURA DE UM OBITO, OU RASTO DE QUE DEIXOU A PESSOA QUE PARTIU

(looking for something or the track left behind by someone who left)

RASTOS DE ALGUEM VIAJOU (PARTIU)

(tracks of someone who left or travelled away)

(missing someone)

SAUDADES -"PIHI WANI PRAU" (DESEJO DE ALGUEM

35

The Outside World and the Yanomami

For the Yanomami, the first significant contact with the outside world came in 1973, when the military government decided to drive the Northern Perimeter highway through Yanomami territory. To build the road, hundreds of workers were brought in by the Camargo Corrêa construction company and its subcontractors. No care was taken to protect Indians from the workers' diseases or their cultural impact. Epidemics of measles and flu, diseases to which the Yanomami have little or no natural immunity, devastated several villages near the road, leading to the reported deaths of 72 per cent of the population in two communities. Furthermore, the miners brought new diseases like TB and significantly increased previous diseases like malaria and onchocerciasis (African river blindness). Indians took to begging at the side of the road and women were used as prostitutes. The road advanced 200 kms before being halted in 1976, when money ran out. The forest cleared for the road never regenerated because smallholders invaded it and used the land for cattle grazing.

In the mid-1970s, wildcat gold miners began invading, culminating in the first fully fledged goldrush in 1987, when thousands poured into the area. The impact of the road had been limited to the villages close to it, but goldmining affected the entire Yanomami territory in Brazil. The *garimpeiros* brought noise, pollution, mercury contamination, violence, guns, alcohol and prostitution with them. They destroyed the self-sufficiency of villages by introducing industrialized foods. But the worst of all the things they brought with them was illness and disease. 'Through prostitution the miners have introduced disease, such as venereal diseases and possibly even AIDS', anthropologist Leslie Sponsel wrote in an article about gold mining and mercury contamination.

By mid-1990 it was reckoned that more than 1,500 Yanomami had died, mostly from malaria and other diseases, but also from gunshot wounds. In May 1988, for instance, four Indians were beaten unconscious and an Indian girl was wounded by leadshot during a conflict with miners.

For Alcida Ramos, the only way to understand how the Yanomami felt about the outsiders who invaded their land is to compare it with earthlings' fear of extra-terrestrial aliens as portrayed in science fiction. Like the aliens, the gold miners demonstrate bizarre and potentially lethal behaviour. For her and other anthropologists, it is the 'colossal cultural misunderstanding' between *garimpeiros* and Yanomami which led not only to the disaster of Haximú but to earlier murders.

Before the *garimpeiros* arrived, the only sounds in the forest were those of parrots squawking, monkeys chattering, the rustling of the branches, the rushing of water over rocks. Ramos graphically describes the change. Evoking a jungle airstrip, she writes of a place:

> where the pandemonium of frenetic machines and airplanes spitting out noises of hell and exhalations of plague recalls Vietnam where red hosepipes, coiled like cobras in the mud, serve as seats for prostitutes and Indians, where guns, alcohol and short tempers combine in Hobbesian scenes and a climate of apocalypse, in this scenario most of the Yanomami had their first encounter with the white man. In this chaos, contrasting and even incompatible modes of being, seeing and wanting mixed in one of the most resounding cultural mismatches in the history of Brazilian indigenism. The consequences could only be tragic.

For the Yanomami the noise, smoke, and strange machines must indeed have seemed like the end of the world, but the only rational explanation for the diseases that began to plague them came from the spirit world. Like all indigenous peoples, they believe that spirits dwell in the natural environment around them. When the forest is attacked, the spirits are attacked and they will want their revenge.

The Spirit World

Davi Kopenawa, who has become the best-known Yanomami leader, is also a shaman. In an interview with Bruce Albert he explained that *Xawara*, a vapour-spirit, is released from the subsoil during mining and brings sickness to both the Yanomami and the *garimpeiros*:

> This thing we call *Xawara* was kept hidden a long time ago by our ancestors. *Omame*, the Yanomami creator-spirit, kept the *Xawara* hidden. He kept it hidden and didn't want the Yanomami to disturb it. He said 'don't touch it!' For this reason he hid it deep in the earth. He also said, 'If this rises to the surface all the Yanomami will start dying in droves!' Having spoken these words, he buried it very deep. But today the *Nabebe*, the whites, after discovering our forests, have been possessed by a frantic desire to take this *Xawara* out from the depths of the earth where *Omame* had hidden it. *Xawara* is also the name by which we call *Booshike*, the substance that you call 'minerals'. We are afraid of it. The *Xawara* is the Yanomami's enemy, and yours too. It

wants to kill us. That way, if you start to get sick, it goes on to kill you. Because of this we Yanomami are very worried.

When the gold stays in the cold depths of the earth, there's no problem. Then everything's just fine. It isn't dangerous. When the whites take the gold out of the earth, they burn it, stir it over the fire as if it were manioc flour. This makes smoke come out of it. This is the way that *Xawara*, which is this smoke from the gold, is created. Afterwards this *Xawara wakexi*, this 'epidemic smoke', spreads not just through the forest, where the Yanomami live, but also through the lands of the whites, everywhere. This is why we are dying – because of this smoke. It becomes measles smoke. It becomes very aggressive and because of this it destroys the Yanomami.

When this smoke reaches the centre of the sky, the sky also begins to get very sick, it also begins to be affected by the *Xawara*. The earth also gets sick. Even the *Hekurabe*, the helper spirits of the shamans, get very sick. Even *Omame* is affected. *Deosime* – God – is too. This is why we are very worried now.

It is not only the Yanomami who are dying. Everyone will die together When the centre of the sky is filled by this smoke it also will begin to die, like a Yanomami. Because of this, when it gets sick the thunder will make itself heard without ceasing. The thunder will get sick too and will bellow with rage, without ceasing, afflicted by the heat

For the Yanomami this means the sky will break, and the many dead Yanomami shamans will want revenge: when the shamans die their Hekurabe, their helper spirits, get very angry. They see that the whites are causing the deaths of the shamans, their 'fathers'. They will want vengeance, they will cut the sky in pieces so that it collapses over the Earth; they will also make the sun fall, and when the sun falls everything will go dark. When the moon and the stars fall, the sky will go dark. We want to tell the whites all this, but they don't listen. They are a different people, and they don't understand

When there are no more Yanomami, then the sky will fall once and for all. When the gold miners have destroyed the Yanomami, no others will spring up in their place, no, none.

Davi and children at Demini   *Fiona Watson/Survival International*

DAVI KOPENAWA

Now in his forties, Davi was born in the Toototobi area and learned Portuguese with Protestant evangelist missionaries. He was employed for ten years by FUNAI as a guide and interpreter for medical teams, and as chief of the post at Watorikitheri. Through the CCPY he began campaigning for the demarcation of the Yanomami area, although FUNAI did not approve of Davi's activities. Once he complained, 'FUNAI doesn't want me to leave my own village, it wants to keep me hidden, it wants me to keep quiet, not to protest, not to talk to others, not to speak to white supporters. [They] forbade me to leave my post, to leave my village. ... But I am not willing to sit still and keep quiet while my people are dying. I need to go out into the world, I need to cry out, I need to protest what is happening. No, not "need", I have the right to spread the news to other countries.' In 1988 he received the UN's Global 500 Award for his contribution to defending the environment.

Davi has taken his cry to Brasília, São Paulo, London, Washington, Oslo, and Vienna. In 1992 he addressed the General Assembly of the UN at a ceremony to mark the opening of the international year of the world's indigenous peoples. After describing the catastrophic effects of the mining, and remembering the helpful intervention of UN Secretary General Javier Pérez de Cuellar in writing to President Collor, and asking his successor

Boutros Boutros Ghali to do the same, Davi told the assembled delegates that he wished to give them a message from *Omame*, the creator of the Yanomami, and the *Shabori*, their shamans. The assembled delegates, more used to the niceties of diplomatic argument, listened to the impassioned plea of the man from the rainforest:

Stop the destruction, stop taking minerals from under the ground and stop building roads through forests. Our word is to protect nature, the wind, the mountains, the forest, the animals and this is what we want to teach you. The leaders of the rich, industrialized world think that they are the owners of the world. But the *Shabori* are the ones who have true knowledge. They are the real first world. And if their knowledge is destroyed, then the white people too will die. It will be the end of the world. This is what we want to avoid.

He also told the UN, 'we are doing all we can to help ourselves. To protect ourselves from white man's disease, we are setting up our own health project. In my region…the river valleys of the Demini, Balawaú and Toototobi, we have 24 villages and a population of 1,048. With the help of government agencies in Canada, Germany, Britain and Switzerland, and NGOs in Britain, Holland, Norway and Brazil, we are setting up a health project that should reach them all. It is the "new partnership" among peoples.'

To leave the rainforest and travel to foreign cities was not easy for a Yanomami. Davi looked at the cities he visited with the eyes of a forest-dweller. Recounting a visit to London, he said:

how strange it all was…so many big buildings. The forest was small and sparse and cut back. So many people! And the noise of the train and the cars. I was sad – such a polluted place, I thought…

I was frightened in England – so much noise and activity, conflicts, thieves. I thought the land was beautiful, but not the buildings. So many people living all on top of one another, 1, 2, 3, 4, 5 storeys, they were like wasps in a wasps' nest!…I thought that to me, the cities were like removing the forest and replacing them with mountains. They're all like that. I thought that it was beautiful, but for me it would be difficult to live there. I liked it that you enjoyed my land, the mountains, the birds singing, the noise of the wind, and of the rain against the trees and the village.

Sometimes Davi compared the poverty he saw in the big cities of the whites with the self-sufficiency of the Yanomami way of life: 'When I go to the big city I see people who are hungry, without anywhere to plant, without drinking water, without anywhere to live. I do not want this to happen to my people too, I do not want them to spoil the forest, which leads to misery.' In an interview with a Brazilian TV station, he said:

> It is not that the Yanomami do not want progress, do not want many of the things that white people have. They want to be able to choose, and not have change thrust upon them, whether they want it or not. I am not saying that I am against progress. I think it is very good when whites come to work amongst the Yanomami to teach reading and writing, how to breed bees, to plant and use medicinal plants, the right way of protecting nature. These white people are very welcome in our land. This for us is progress. What we do not want are the mining companies, which destroy the forest, and the *garimpeiros*, who bring so many diseases. These whites must respect our Yanomami land. The *garimpeiros* bring guns, alcohol, and prostitution and destroy all the nature wherever they go. The machines throw oil into the rivers and kill the life in them and the people and animals that depend on them. For us, this is not progress. We want progress without destruction. We want to study, to learn new ways of cultivating the land, living from its fruits. The Yanomami do not want to live from dealing with money, with gold, we are not prepared for this. We need time to learn ... we do not want to live without trees, hunting, fish and clean water. If this happens misery will come to our people.

Shamans

For the Yanomami the shaman, or spiritual leader, has the job of interpreting the world around them, making sense of what is happening, whether it is illness or invasion, through his knowledge of, and communication with, the spirits. Only the shaman knows how to use the plants with hallucinogenic properties that enable travel to the spirit world, only he has the power to speak to the spirits, the *Hekura* and the *Shabori*, to see them and turn into them. The spirits can be friendly or hostile. It is the shaman's job to call on spirits that cure diseases, rather than cause them, avert storms rather than create them, and bring success rather than failure to hunting expeditions.

It is also his job to see off spirits sent by hostile shamans, and if necessary take the offensive and send spirits from his community to warring communities to provoke catastrophes. He will regularly call the spirit helpers from the level above earth (there are four layers in the Yanomami cosmos) down to the Yanomami level.

41

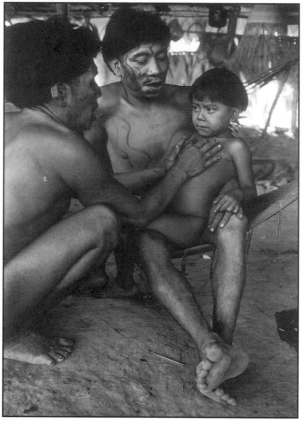

A shaman examines
a sick child

Victor Englebert 1980/
Survival International

There are other spirits, which cannot be controlled by the shaman: the harmful spirits of the forest, the *Ne Waribe*, dangerous to encounter and ugly to look at. They are the spirits which live in specific places, such as a hill or thicket, or in the rain, or in the night. They are threatening because they are believed to have the same attitude towards the Yanomami as the Yanomami have towards the game they hunt.

Sometimes the Yanomami use plants and herbs to cure common ailments. The leaves of the jacaranda tree are rubbed into a snakebite, the bark of the cinchona tree (from which quinine comes) is used for eye infections and

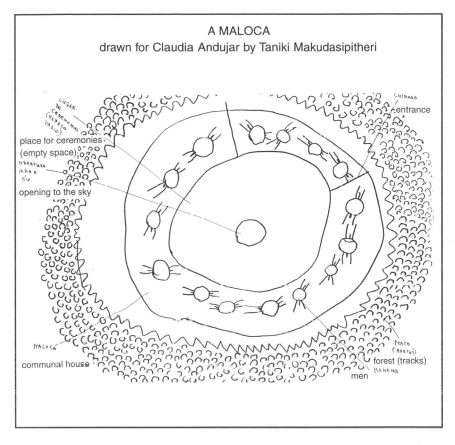

A MALOCA
drawn for Claudia Andujar by Taniki Makudasipitheri

vomiting – although nowadays western medicines are considered more efficient. But the main method of curing all sickness is shamanism. Shamanism is more powerful because it is believed that it destroys the supernatural cause of the disease and the agent of the disease, the hostile spirit. Plant cures are more often used after the cause has been eradicated by the shamanic session.

There are four main causes of disease in the Yanomami world: 'sorcery' from allies or enemies; *Hekura* sent by a distant hostile shaman; harm done to a person's 'animal double' (all Yanomami are twinned with animals from birth, so if an animal is injured by a hunter in the forest then its Yanomami counterpart will also fall ill, or even die); and an attack from hostile spirits in the forest.

43

THE CREATION ACCORDING TO THE YANOMAMI

The Yanomami myth of the creation begins with the sky falling on to the earth, after a great shaman died, which caused most people to be thrown into the underworld. Some Yanomami tried to escape the falling sky, and when their parrot made a hole in the sky by scraping it with his beak, they escaped through it.

They then found a forest and planted gardens, had children and multiplied but then disappeared…The first people kept changing like the forest kept changing. The people who were created first were transformed into animals when this earth was created; they became parrots, cutias, tapirs and alligators. The macaws, the red deer, the jaguars, the toucans, the sloths, the armadillos that we see today are those people who were transformed in those days and spread out in all directions like game. In the beginning there weren't any animals. The meat that we eat today is from those people who were turned into animals, from those animal ancestors.

Those people didn't know much about anything. They didn't bury the ashes of their bones. They used to eat each other; every time one of them was transformed, they killed him to eat him, in the same way that we eat game. They didn't perform a ceremonial dialogue for the ash of the bones, they didn't go into mourning; they only ate each other. So that was how our animal ancestors lived, in their ignorance. In the end they disappeared. We who are here today were created by *Omame* and it was he who taught us the right way to live.

Source: Ikahi Yanomami, recorded by Bruce Albert, in Survival International Newsletter, No.27

The Yanomami and the Land

Like all indigenous peoples, the Yanomami's attachment to their land is deep, spiritual and essential to their well-being. It involves much more than liking a place they have always lived on, or that is fertile and full of game. Davi Kopenawa explains the concept of *Urihi:*

> *Urihi* for us means our place, our land. This *Urihi* Yanomami is not for sale. *Urihi* has no price at all. There is no money that can pay for the Yanomami's land. The Yanomami already looked after this earth long before any politicians arrived. Our communities don't have paper. Our paper is our thoughts, our beliefs. Our 'paper' is very ancient; we

Pounding timbó leaves   *Fiona Watson/Survival International*

had it long before the white people arrived and wanted to take our
Urihi. Our thought is different from yours. We destroy only a bit of
forest to work, to plant. We do not cut down trees to sell. We cut with
the permission of the community. We plant food to sustain the
community.

The CCPY Education Project

In July 1995 the CCPY (Pro-Yanomami Commission) opened a school in
Demini, in which the age of the 80 pupils ranged from nine to sixty-one.
They learned how to read and write in Yanomami. Some have since become
teachers in other villages, others want to become health agents and heads of
post. The most advanced pupils will go on to Boa Vista to study Portuguese.
The education project is funded by several European NGOs, including an
eight-year commitment from the Norwegian Rainforest Foundation. In a
letter to Norwegian schoolchildren who are raising money for the school,
the Yanomami pupils said:

45

We want to put our thoughts down on paper so they can be properly understood.

We are learning to write our own Yanomami language, because before we didn't know how to write. Now it is a teacher from the other people who has been teaching us. After we have learned we will have our own teachers and it will be our turn to teach those who live further away. This is why we, the young people, are learning to write. But you, the other people, mustn't worry and think: 'Won't the Yanomami become white people?' Because what we want is to defend our land. We don't want to waste this campaign because we don't want to fool you other people.

This is the first time we are sending a message to you and now you, other people, can look at these words. At our school we, the young people, we also want to be able to cure each other. Three of us are learning to use a microscope. They identify the malaria sickness so that when we get ill we ourselves can treat it and get well.

We want to do this among ourselves and this will make us happy, also because you, the other people, have helped us.

5

THE GOLD RUSH

The Amazon gold rush in the 1980s involved more people and produced more gold than the nineteenth-century Klondike and California booms combined. It was the Yanomami's misfortune to be living in one of the richest gold areas. More than a million wildcat prospectors poured into the Amazon basin region during the decade. They came mostly from the impoverished Northeast, but men and women from every state in Brazil could be found among them. At the height of the boom perhaps one-third of the entire Amazon population was involved in some way or another in the gold rush. Working as cooks, pilots, shopkeepers, gold buyers, taxi drivers and prostitutes, they serviced and supplied the gold miners.

The boom had its roots in the military regime's policy towards the Amazon, which was seen as an 'empty' wilderness that needed to be occupied, and its development policy in general, which was producing hordes of landless small farmers, ousted from their holdings by the building of giant dams and by the mechanization needed to produce huge harvests of soybeans for export to the European animal-feed market. Traditionally, the evicted small farmers had made for the cities to swell the shanty towns. The military government decided instead to lure them to the Amazon, first with the promise of land, then with the opening up of the goldfields. The military had become aware of the fantastic mineral wealth that lay under the rainforest in 1975 after Radam, the first aerial survey of the region, had been concluded. The discovery coincided with soaring gold prices on the international markets. From US$150 at the beginning of the 1970s, the price of an ounce of gold had risen to US$900 by 1980. The lure was irresistible.

In the late 1980s, a third factor fuelled the gold rush: the economic policy of the first non-military president in 21 years, José Sarney. His government's radical anti-inflation measures led labour and capital to flee to the informal mining sector where controls and taxes were ignored and cash was the currency. In short, the Amazon – just a few days' bus journey away from the poor cities of the Northeast – became Eldorado, where fortunes could be made, where the key to the good life could be found by use of the only asset most Brazilians possessed – a capacity for hard work. 'No other factor has produced so large a migration of people to the Brazilian Amazon in so short a time as gold fever', recorded a UN document. Almost overnight, goldmining

47

had become a major economic activity in the world's largest remaining rainforest.

Each year of the boom, 100 tonnes of gold were extracted from the Amazon region. That was the conservative estimate of a miners' union. But this massive wealth contributed very little to the region's development, as most was removed from the region, and was also unregistered and therefore untaxed, so the revenue gained by the local authorities was absurdly small.

Roraima

In his book, *At the End of the Rainbow*, Gordon MacMillan explained why Roraima became the centre of the gold rush. Because of its location on the edge of the ancient geological formation known as the Guiana Shield, Roraima was discovered to be a particularly mineral-rich state: it had not only gold, diamonds and cassiterite in river sediments but radioactive minerals such as tantalite, molybdenum, columbite and ilmenite. But the mineral-rich areas were difficult to get at; most were located in the heart of the territory that has been inhabited by the Yanomami for centuries and who were still, even in the 1970s, largely isolated from contact with the outside world.

Not only was it Indian territory, but there were no roads. This did not daunt the military, who set about providing roads. First they began driving the ambitious Northern Perimeter Highway through the rainforest inhabited by the Yanomami, from east to west. Then they began another road, the BR174, running north from Manaus, to meet it. Both roads cut through heavily forested areas, the refuge of the Yanomami and, in the case of the BR174, the equally untouched Waimiri-Atroari.

Unlike the more accessible southern Amazon, Roraima, located as it is in the far north of the Amazon region, was too remote to attract tax incentives and venture capital for cattle and agricultural projects. But when it came to gold, there were several factors that helped to make it especially attractive to prospectors. The gold was mostly to be found in the beds and banks of the rivers, which made it easier to get at, and it could be mined with rudimentary technology. Roraima's dry season conveniently coincided with the wet season elsewhere in the Amazon, when mining became impossible.

Supplementing their income by alternative means was a traditional practice for small farmers in the Amazon, who collected Brazil nuts, migrated to help with a rice harvest, or prospected for gold. Roraima now had a large contingent of small farmers, as the road building programme had stimulated migration. As part of the policy of bringing 'people without land' from the overcrowded

A highway cuts through Roraima rainforest

*Victor Englebert 1980/
Survival International*

Northeast to the 'land without people' of the Amazon basin, several colonization projects had been started. Yet without proper infrastructure, or the aid of extension workers or any form of credit or subsidy, they limped along at subsistence level until the gold rush began. Nearly the entire population of smallholders abandoned the daily toil of the land for the adventure of the *garimpo*. Cows were sold to finance the trip, and food production declined. Between 1985 and 1990 there was a 34 per cent drop in the area planted with the four main crops – banana, manioc, maize and rice – while at the same time Roraima's population, and the concomitant demand for food, expanded by 73 per cent. Much had to be flown or trucked in, inflating food prices.

Many of the amateur gold prospectors returned from the camps in the forest too sick with malaria to work the land. Some lost everything. But many made enough for their efforts to seem worthwhile. Even as little as 20 grammes of gold a month meant cash in hand, which subsistence farming did not provide. It was enough to buy a fridge or to pay off a debt. Gordon MacMillan concluded that informal-sector mining made good sense for smallholders in the Amazon: 'As long as this remains the case, pressure on mineral-rich indigenous lands like the Yanomami will continue'.

At least half the *garimpeiros* came from a farming background, whether in Roraima or elsewhere. There is no escaping the fact that one of the few economically viable options open to both the rural and the urban poor in Brazil is gold prospecting, and for the vast majority whether it is in indigenous land is totally irrelevant. By the late 1970s they were pouring into Roraima at a rate of 200 per day. The population doubled to 80,000 during the 1970s, and by 1991 it had reached 215,000. Three-quarters of the men came from the Northeast, sixty per cent from one state alone – Maranhão – where absentee landlords held most of the land and dirt poor villages subsisted in feudal conditions without electricity, running water or sewerage, the children condemned to illiteracy. Many had already left the land to look for work in the towns. For them the *garimpo* represented life's single chance of making good, of striking it rich. That chance, however slight, outweighed all the risks.

As outsiders flocked to Boa Vista, Roraima's capital, situated on the western bank of the River Branco, it mushroomed from a sleepy, dusty, one-horse settlement to become the base and supplier for mining activities involving up to 40,000 people. In the feverish frontier town street after street was given over to gold shops, bars, brothels and stores selling prospectors' equipment: hammocks, mosquito nets, knives, primus stoves, cooking pots, boots. Consumption was conspicuous. Successful prospectors swaggered down the streets sporting chunky gold chains and bracelets and mouthfuls of glittering gold teeth.

Scores of single-engine planes and helicopters crowded the runways of Boa Vista's airport and the other clandestine airstrips scattered around the ranches of the savannah. For a while, Boa Vista's modest airport became the third busiest in the country, surpassed only by Rio de Janeiro and São Paulo, and commercial airlines had to take extra precautions to avoid collisions with the hundreds of Cessnas and Pipers taking off and landing at all hours. The streets where the gold buyers and sellers were concentrated expanded to fill entire blocks. On the town's outskirts, where herds of capybara had once roamed, the clumps of *buriti* palms disappeared as huts and houses spread. The rapid, unplanned urbanization brought violence and alcoholism: murders became frequent. In a town where traffic lights were still unknown, traffic accidents multiplied.

The focus of the prospectors' activities was the Yanomami reserve. Without roads – the Perimeter Highway had been abandoned and was now overgrown – the only way to reach the rivers deep inside the Yanomami area was to fly in. An incessant traffic of small planes dangerously crammed with drums of

Boa Vista gold shops

Fiona Watson

diesel oil, food supplies and armed *garimpeiros* flew to and from the clandestine airstrips hacked out of the forest inside the Yanomami reserve. Once inside, their only contact was by radio. The airwaves crackled with messages for the *garimpeiros* from their wives, girlfriends, mothers and partners, demanding news, money, advising of the birth of new children, of deaths and illness in the family, warning of shady deals, of guns on the way, of double-crossing. Although everyone was engaged in an illegal activity – invading an indigenous area – there were never any warnings about the police or the authorities, because there was no need.

In the *garimpos*, grammes of gold were the only currency that mattered. For much of the time, a gramme was worth about US$10. A kilo of sugar, salt, rice or beans cost three- to four-tenths of a gramme, or US$4, twice to four times the normal price. A can of beer cost half a gramme, a packet of cigarettes one gramme. An airdrop of supplies cost 200 grammes.

Gordon MacMillan calculated that only a small elite became rich from gold and allied activities, for example from charging landing fees at airstrips. Between 400 and 1000 individuals, no more than 1 to 2.5 per cent of the total, got rich, accumulating over 5 kg of gold. Probably no more than ten became millionaires, extracting over 100 kg of gold. Those who made money usually bought ranches. One of this lucky minority was a *garimpo* pilot who operated an air taxi company and ran mining operations. After acquiring approximately 120 kg of gold from Yanomami lands between 1986 and 1989, he bought two large ranches and supplied his own beef to the men in his mining camps.

The money produced by the gold rush also fuelled crime: drink, drugs and weapons were all easy to come by, and fights, many of them fatal, were frequent. Mining operations offered a convenient cover for the distribution, and occasionally the processing of drugs. For the cocaine dealers, gold had a definite advantage over US dollars, because it could not be traced. Women were another cause of violence. Only the larger camps in the Amazon had brothels, many with under-age prostitutes recruited in the towns. The smaller camps had women cooks, many of whom topped up their earnings with paid sex. Professional prostitutes were not common in Roraima mining camps.

GARIMPEIRO LIFE

'Attention Pedro Queiros, better known as Itaituba at the Swollen Feet Airstrip: let me know if you received the revolver.'

'Attention Adão, better known as Old Negro in the Upper Mucujai: your wife Raimunda says she's had the baby: it's a boy. They are both well and you must send some gold.'

'Attention Ernandes, better known as Rich Mouth: your wife Olga says the man you sent with the five grammes of gold on Monday didn't deliver it. He sold it and spent the money and only delivered your letter. Everton is no better and there's no money to pay for a doctor. She doesn't know what to do and she's losing her patience.'

Every day Humberto Campos, the announcer at Radio Roraima in Boa Vista, reads out over 200 messages like these. Each costs 12 cruzados – about 80 pence – and broadcast at the rate of up to 1,500 a week, they have become the radio's main source of income. One day's messages brings in more than a month's normal advertising.

In one shop in Boa Vista I met Raimundo Nonato dos Santos, just back from the gold rush front with his precious store of gold dust. He unscrewed the top of a plastic medicine bottle and carefully tipped a few grains of gold on to the scales: 35.5 grammes at 107 cruzados. That meant 3,798 cruzados (£470) altogether – 10 times the minimum salary – what most Brazilians earn – for a month's work. But tomorrow the price would probably be better,

---

so he recapped his gold dust and put it away in his haversack. Thirty-five grammes was the result of 48 days' work and Raimundo reckoned it would buy food for 20 days, for him, his wife, four children and mother-in-law.

Aged 38, Raimundo had arrived from one of Brazil's poorest states, Piauí, a year ago. It had taken him 14 days travelling by bus, boat and finally plane to get to Boa Vista.

'I heard you could "enrich" here quickly. I hung around the airport till I fixed up a ride on a plane with some other men. We went to Paapiú and I began working with 10 other men in a grotto' – the *garimpeiros*' name for a riverbank, which they break down with high pressure jets of water, driven by a pump.

'The food is terrible, just beans, flour and rice. Lots of men get malaria but I'm lucky I've never had it. At night there are vampire bats that suck your blood if you haven't got a mosquito net on your hammock. The Indians? They like us, they say "*garimpeiro amigo*".'

Jan Rocha, *The Guardian*, 18 November 1989

By the end of the 1980s Roraima was producing 10 per cent of all the gold extracted in the Brazilian Amazon, although the sector remained totally informal: work contracts were verbal, incomes undeclared, taxes unpaid. Labour relations were unprotected by law, but, unlike other Amazon activities, they were not debt-dependent. The wealth produced by the gold flowed unchecked through Boa Vista to Rio, São Paulo and abroad. No serious attempt was made to control it. When Inland Revenue inspectors did check the cargoes of light planes one day they found no less than 30 kg of gold. Yet during the height of the Roraima boom in 1988-89, only 15 tonnes were registered, less than one-third of the likely output. Only 33 of Boa Vista's many gold dealers were legally registered.

As the dealers burned off the mercury from the little lumps of amalgam hidden in little medicine flasks brought to them by the *garimpeiros*, to reveal the gold, clouds of mercury vapour filled the air of the town, adding yet another negative effect of the gold rush on the environment: air pollution.

Boa Vista's authorities erected a giant concrete statue of a *garimpeiro* in the middle of the central plaza. In the best style of a heroic Soviet worker, it towers above the trees. It is one of Brazil's few statues of a worker rather than of a general or president. Symbolically, the statue dominates the square around which the authorities of the state, the governor, the legislative assembly, the courts (and the bishop) have their palaces.

Illegal prospectors' landing strip,
upper Mucajaí river, Roraima

Charles Vincent/
Survival International

The prosecutors investigating the Haximú massacre described how local society viewed *garimpeiros* and Indians:

Historically the *garimpeiros* are seen as largely responsible for the foundation and consolidation of the town of Boa Vista and the territory of Roraima. The *garimpeiro* was a tamer of the wild, a pioneer, courageous, strong. The historic concept of non-indigenous society was so favourable that it judged him worthy of a monumental statue in the heart of Boa Vista.

54

The *garimpeiros* had not only changed Roraima out of all recognition, they had acquired unrivalled knowledge of the local subsoil. As MacMillan wrote, 'a greater knowledge of the state's subsoil is currently retained in the minds of *garimpeiros* than is available in any published documents'.

The Invasion of the Yanomami Area

At first it was cassiterite, or tin, rather than gold that drew the prospectors into the Yanomami area. Almost immediately the presence of white men carrying influenza and measles, diseases to which the Yanomami have no natural immunity, caused sickness and death among the Indians. In response, in 1975 FUNAI expelled 500 miners and prospectors. In 1979 the military government's survey company, DOCEGEO, confirmed the existence of 15,000 tonnes of high-grade ore in the Yanomami area, but warned that the economic benefits would not outweigh the potentially damaging effects on the Indians' health and culture. In 1985, defying the authorities, a self-styled leader of the prospectors called José Altino Machado, who had migrated to Roraima from the state of Minas Gerais in the south, led an airborne invasion. Sixty prospectors in five planes flew to Surucucus to claim the cassiterite mine there. There was an outcry and they were summarily expelled. But as gold prices leapt from 1986, prospectors abandoned their interest in cassiterite and set off to find gold. Pressure to open up the Yanomami reserve grew.

The Yanomami themselves quickly picked up mining techniqes and began to barter gold for more useful things such as hammocks, knives, pots and fishhooks. The growing presence of the *garimpeiros*, however, presented the Yanomami with a cultural dilemma. Traditionally the Yanomami's relationships fell into two distinct categories: ceremonial for strangers or distant communities, informal for those they knew well. Missionaries and anthropologists who had lived with them for a long time fell into the category of close neighbours with whom they developed mutually acceptable bartering practices. But no mechanism existed for dealing with strange, not necessarily friendly, white predators who came and went. They fell into a new, ill-understood category, and no etiquette existed for dealing with them. Anthropologist Alcida Ramos explained the problem the *garimpeiros* posed for the Yanomami:

> They are strangers, but at the same time they are not such infrequent visitors that nothing can be exchanged with them, nor are they intimate whites who can be treated informally. However, barter is done with the *garimpeiros* because both parties desire to acquire goods, food and

services. Under such circumstances, transactions of this sort could only be carried out under the protective shield of ceremonial dialogues. But in the absence of this common code, they are naked, unprotected by any symbolic lightning conductor that could prevent situations in which the participants are totally exposed to the ultimate consequences of whatever tensions or misunderstandings might arise.

For their part the *garimpeiros*, ignorant of these cultural complexities, are guided only by the logic of wealth accumulation in its crudest form, that is, to get rich quick.

Anthropologist Bruce Albert describes how the colossal, and, in many cases tragic, misunderstanding between the Indians and the *garimpeiros* evolves:

When they install themselves in a new site within the Yanomami area, to begin with the *garimpeiros* arrive in small groups. As they are few they feel vulnerable before the Indians. Fearing a negative reaction from the Indians, they try to buy their approval with a generous distribution of goods and food. For their part, the Indians have little or no experience with Whites and take this attitude as an expression of the generosity that can be expected of any group that wants to establish links for intercommunity alliances.

While this cultural misunderstanding is unfolding, the Indians have not yet felt the impact of mining activities on their health and their environment. In their eyes the work of the gold miners still seems something enigmatic and irrelevant. With irony, condescendingly, they call them the 'earth eaters' and compare them to a band of wild hogs snuffling in the mud.

Later the number of *garimpeiros* increases substantially and the initial generosity is no longer necessary. The Indians are no longer a threat but a nuisance with their insistent demands for the goods they have become used to getting. The *garimpeiros* get irritated and try to drive them away from the mining areas with false promises of future presents and with impatient and aggressive attitudes.

By now the Indians have begun to feel a rapid deterioration in their health and diet. The rivers are polluted, the game has disappeared, and many people begin to die because of the constant epidemics of malaria, influenza and so on, so that the economic and social life of the communities becomes destructured. This leads the Indians to see

Evidence of the effect on the Yanomami of the prospectors' presence: a traditional *maloca* covered with plastic sheeting   *Charles Vincent/ Survival International*

the goods and food of the *garimpeiros* as a vital and unquestionable compensation for the destruction that has been caused. When this compensation is denied them, in their understanding a situation of explicit hostility has been created.

In this way a stalemate is created: the Indians become dependent on the *garimpeiros* at the exact moment that they no longer need to buy the Indians' goodwill. This paradox is at the root of all the conflicts involving Indians and *garimpeiros* in the Yanomami area. It opens up the possibility of the smallest incident degenerating into open conflict. As the difference in force between the *garimpeiros* and the Indians is enormous, the Yanomami always come off worse in terms of violence.

This sort of situation clearly shows up to what point the logic of the goldmining economy repels not only the participation of the Indians but even their mere presence. The *garimpeiros* who use mechanized techniques have no interest in the Indians, not even as labour. At the least they are an inconvenience, at the worst they are a threat to the miners' safety. If they cannot drive them away with presents and promises, then the solution is to intimidate them, or to exterminate them.

Clashes

The first serious clash came in 1987, when four Yanomami and a *garimpeiro* were killed on the Mucajaí river. The prospectors had tried to claim a site already being worked by the Indians. This led to a half-hearted attempt to remove the *garimpeiros* in September of that year. But the failure of the operation revealed that not only was the political will to remove prospectors lacking, but also that gold fever had contaminated officials themselves at all levels. The same year, the Association of Gold Miners of Boa Vista published a communiqué signed by over 1,000 gold miners, stating: 'We are not afraid of the police, or of FUNAI. We are not going to abandon the region. We have political guarantees that the army and the air force will not intervene. We have the support of the business class of Roraima that we will not be removed from the goldmining areas'.

Unable or unwilling to expel the gold miners, FUNAI instead banned health-workers, missionaries and anthropologists from the area. In other words, in an extraordinary inversion of their duty to protect the Indians, they expelled anyone who might have acted as an independent observer of the *garimpeiros*' disastrous impact on the Yanomami. The Yanomami were left completely alone to face the disruption, destruction and disease brought by the invaders. Worse still, FUNAI also abandoned its own role of providing medical assistance to the Indians. Staff were withdrawn from the airstrip and post at Paapiú, which was left to became the *garimpeiros*' staging post for reaching more remote areas. The gold miners were now effectively in control of the Yanomami area, and they began using the airstrips that had been built by the army, by the Roraima government, and by American evangelical missionaries. They also opened up scores of new airstrips in forested areas.

By the end of 1987, bands of *garimpeiros* were well established at the headwaters of the Mucajaí, the Apiaú and the Couto de Magalhães, three important rivers inside the Yanomami reserve. From 1986 to 1992, over 200 *garimpos*, or prospecting sites, were worked. In 1988 President Sarney announced that the Yanomami territory was to be cut up and divided into 19 separate 'islands', surrounded by areas designated 'national forest', where mining would be legal. A similar idea, involving 15 islands in Roraima and six in Amazonas, had been devised and mooted in 1978 by FUNAI itself. It meant that groups of Yanomami villages would now be separated from each

58

Garimpeiros in Roraima   *Fiona Watson*

other by areas of no-man's land in which the *garimpeiros* would hold sway. At the stroke of the president's pen, the Yanomami's traditionally recognized area of over nine million hectares had been reduced by almost three-quarters, to 2.4 million hectares, in order to benefit the mining lobby.

Garimpeiros and Votes

The interests of the informal mining sector quickly came to dominate the state of Roraima, both politically and economically. As the gold rush gathered momentum it swept everyone along. Anyone who had a bit of capital invested in it for a quick return. Around the *garimpeiros* ancillary services sprang up – entertainment, bars, brothels, boarding houses, restaurants and taxi firms.

But the prospectors were also electors. After two decades of military rule, Brazil had, in 1985, once again become a constitutional democracy, where the vote counted. In 1990 Roraima, until then a federally-run territory with a governor chosen in Brasília, had become Brazil's 25th state. This meant that the population had the right to elect their own governor, three senators and eight federal congressional deputies. With a contingent of up to 40,000 votes, the *garimpeiros* outnumbered any other sector of the population, and their vote was courted by all the candidates. Although by definition the informal mining sector was beyond the reach of government authority, every candidate for political power in Roraima made the *garimpeiro* cause their own. The right to mine in indigenous areas became the central issue in Roraima politics. The fact that it been definitively declared illegal under the new constitution of 1988 seemed to be neither here nor there in the world of Roraima realpolitik.

Instead, mining and politics became a two-way traffic. *Garimpeiro* leaders and mine-owners ran for political office while members of the existing local political class invested in mining and therefore defended what had become their own interest too. Any moral qualms about defending an illegal activity – mining inside indigenous areas – were neatly overcome by classifying mineral resources on Indian lands as common property. In any case, for most of the electorate defending the right to mine in indigenous areas meant the politician was committed to the progress and development of Roraima, whereas attempts to stop the mining were perceived as threats against progress. So at least four state deputies, one senator, and one federal deputy were financing mining operations inside the Yanomami reserve between 1987 and 1990, as were top officials in the state administration. These included the head of the state police force, the secretary for transport and, incredibly, the secretary for the environment.

For some, success in the illegal Roraima gold mines opened the door to political success on the national stage. Elton Rohnelt, an adventurer from the southern state of Rio Grande do Sul once caught smuggling arms at Boa Vista airport, moved from being the owner of a fleet of planes running supplies to the *garimpeiros* to become head of the state government's mining department, the most senior authority over mining in Roraima. Even more ironically, he later became state secretary for the environment, while his daughter was appointed secretary for tourism. In 1994 he was elected to the national congress, representing one of the parties supporting President Fernando Henrique Cardoso. In 1996 he became a government leader in Congress, and worked hard to push through a bill to allow mining in Indian reserves, effectively overriding the Brazilian constitution's protection of these lands.

Antonio Dias, who had become a wealthy man through selling equipment for *garimpeiro* activites, was Roraima's vice-governor. Another man who used *garimpeiro* support to reach high places was Romero Jucá, an economist from the north-eastern state of Pernambuco. Chosen by President Sarney to head FUNAI, as part of the region's quota of jobs in the federal government, he had been accused of taking bribes to allow illegal logging on an indigenous reserve in the state of Mato Grosso. This did not stop him being appointed

Roraima's last nominated governor in 1988, when he made goldminers' interests his priority. After his term as governor, Jucá was elected to Congress. His wife, who had also acquired a taste for political life, got herself elected senator for Roraima.

The rapid growth in economic importance of the minerals sector saw the Amazon mining lobby emerge as a powerful force on both the regional and national stage. The region, traditionally seen as remote and outside mainstream political and economic affairs, acquired a new importance. Amazon politicians, once dismissed as backward, often exotic, figures, now carried a certain weight in national and even international politics.

The Death Toll

The gold rush swept on. Non governmental organizations such as the CCPY and Survival, banned from entering the area, could only guess at what was happening. But as more and more Yanomami with malaria and malnutrition turned up at the Casa do Indio, the Indian hospital in Boa Vista, and the death toll mounted, realization grew that a disaster was taking place. The hospital was filled with sick men, women and children, many of them brought in by *garimpeiros* themselves, who had been moved by their plight.

Health officials were surprised at the extent of the malnutrition they saw among the Yanomami. Normally self-sufficient in food, even taking into account the poor soils of the rainforest, the Yanomami fed themselves well. But the *garimpeiros*' arrival disrupted their natural harmony with their surroundings and with food.

Upon first moving into an area, *garimpeiros* usually gave Indians handouts of food in order to placate them. In response to this free food many Indians had abandoned planting crops. When the *garimpeiros* had established themselves in the area they stopped donating food, and the Indians began to suffer from malnutrition and even starvation.

Malaria was not altogether unknown in the Yamomami lands before the *garimpeiros* moved in. But gold mining uses pieces of equipment that quickly become filled with rainwater, and creates stagnant ponds caused by draining and dredging. These are the ideal conditions – stale, unmoving water – under which mosquitoes breed. Many *garimpeiros* were already malarial before they entered Yanomami lands, and after biting the gold miners mosquitoes spread the disease easily, both to other *garimpeiros* and the Yanomami. But the Yanomami did not have regular health care or treatment for the disease.

The Brazilian and international press published pictures of desperately emaciated and dying Indians. The outcry at last moved the government to

The emergency airlift   *Charles Vincent/Survival International*

attempt to remedy its criminal neglect of the Yanomami. In 1989 an emergency health programme was set up and army helicopters began to airlift sick Indians to hospitals in Boa Vista. The very organizations meant to help the Indians and which the government had banned from the area were now asked to step in and save the Indians. For many it was too late: an estimated 1,500, or 15 per cent of the entire Yanomami population in Brazil, died as a direct or indirect result of the gold rush.

It was a terrible illustration of the global economy at its worst: the true cost of fluctuating commodity values, in both human and ecological terms, is seldom recognized and virtually never accounted for, as Gordon MacMillan put it. Yet still President Sarney resisted the intense international pressure to expel the *garimpeiros*. By now the formal mining sector was alarmed, as the gold flowed out of the rivers of the Yanomami area. One of the biggest Brazilian companies, Paranapanema, lobbied to have the *garimpos* closed. But it was only when Fernando Collor was elected to succeed Sarney in December 1989 that action was taken.

Collor came to power at a moment when environmental issues had suddenly acquired global importance. Environmental policy was now a factor taken into account by the World Bank and other multilateral agencies considering loans for development. Collor realized that saving the Yanomami was not only an environmentally friendly thing to do, but that it would also bring him useful international credibility. The fate of the Yanomami had become the yardstick of the Brazilian government's commitment to protecting the environment. Collor ordered the removal of the *garimpeiros*.

A man who liked flamboyant gestures, Collor wanted the operation to be carried out in as dramatic a way as possible. He travelled up to the Yanomami area himself, donning jungle camouflage uniform. Federal police agents were drafted into Roraima from all over Brazil, and teams of them travelled into the Yanomami reserve, blowing up jungle airstrips and ferrying out *garimpeiros*. But many of the more experienced gold miners hid in the forest, repaired the airstrips and carried on mining once the police had moved on. Only later on in 1990, when the police began destroying the machinery as well as the airstrips, was the mining brought to a halt.

In November 1991, just six months before Brazil hosted the United Nations Conference on Environment and Development (UNCED), also known as the Earth Summit, the biggest environmental conference ever held, the government announced the formal creation of a Yanomami reserve covering 9.4 million hectares. The Summit was held in Rio de Janeiro, where thousands of environmentalists from every country in the world debated every conceivable topic and over 100 heads of state made speeches and signed conventions. For the Summit delegates, the Indians were the heroes and gold miners the villains. Among the resolutions and measures the Summit produced was Agenda 21, an ambitious list of measures to protect the environment and indigenous peoples.

But once again, as happens so often in Brazil, fortunes swiftly changed. After the Earth Summit, the environment sank from view as an issue in Brazilian politics and the police blockade of the Yanomami reserve collapsed. What is more, by the end of that year, 1992, Collor had resigned from office, minutes before Congress began to vote on his impeachment for corruption. By early 1993 as many as 12,000 *garimpeiros* were back inside the Yanomami reserve. FUNAI, with its budget slashed by over 80 per cent as part of the general government austerity cuts, was impotent to stop the re-invasion. The *garimpeiros* were impatient to make up for lost time. With Collor gone, they no longer feared expulsion or harassment. In July 1993 the Haximú massacre took place.

6

BRAZIL'S OFFICIAL INDIAN POLICY

'Everywhere the Indian has tried to stop the locomotive of progress he has been run down, massacred and decimated', said the late Darcy Ribeiro, one of Brazil's most eminent anthropologists. The process began as soon as the white men arrived 500 years ago. Brazil was not an empty land. It was inhabited by large nations of indigenous peoples, hunting, fishing, gathering and planting, sometimes making alliances, sometimes making war against each other.

Over the next four hundred years millions of Indians were slaughtered or enslaved. The survivors fled or were driven back from the coast to the Mato Grosso and the Amazon region. Occasionally, for example during a nationalist upsurge, the Indians were romanticized in literature or music as 'noble savages', the original Brazilians. Carlos Gomes' 1870 opera *O Guarani* is the most famous example. But even in the first half of the twentieth century 80 tribes were completely wiped out after contact with white society.

In the 1950s, 100 years after the wagons in the United States headed west and the great tribes of the plains fought their last battles before being confined to reservations, Brazilians began their own march to the west. The Americans laid railways, the Brazilians built roads, but the result was the same for the Indians who were in the way. In many indigenous communities missionaries, first Catholic, later increasingly Protestant, often opened the way, deliberately or unwittingly, for "development". In the 1970s the assault began on the indigenous tribes' last haven, the Amazon region. The Amazon was home to the largest groups living in the biggest areas: the Tucano, the Tikuna, the Urueu Wau-Wau, the Suruí, the Waimiri Atroari, the Yanomami. The military, steeped in nationalist sentiment, saw the vast, sparsely populated region as Brazil's vulnerable Achilles heel, coveted by other nations because of its immense natural resources. They wanted to tame it with roads and towns, explore its mineral wealth, harness its hydroelectric powers, occupy it. The World Bank bought the dream and made loans for roads to help create a well-populated, urban Amazon.

Once again the indigenous communities were in the way and had to be dealt with. FUNAI, the government's Indian agency, set up to replace the scandal-ridden Indian Protection Service (SPI), behaved like the instrument of a colonial power which did not believe in self-determination for its indigenous peoples. The indigenous communities were never consulted about what was happening, they were simply told. Indian policy is still decided in Brasília by the government of the day without consultation. Laws affecting Indian communities are passed in a Congress that has no indigenous representatives. Only once has an Indian been elected to Congress. Not so long ago indigenous leaders who merely tried to enter the Congress building were barred for not wearing ties.

Individual FUNAI employees have often been knowledgeable, dedicated men and women doing their best to protect the communities from disease and exploitation. But the men who run the agency have usually been appointed for political reasons, without any previous experience or indeed sympathy for Indian affairs: military officers by the military regime, lawyers and economists by civilian governments.

Brazil's 1988 constitution recognized the rights of the 300,000 or so Indians who remain after 500 years of slaughter and persecution, except for the vital right to own their own land. Drawn up to restore the civil liberties taken away by the generals, the constitution recognizes the right of the indigenous communities to their own social organization, customs, languages, beliefs, traditions and their original rights over the lands they traditionally occupy, but not their right to use and dispose of these lands as they might think fit. Indigenous people can benefit from the fruits of their land, but ultimate ownership rests with the federal government. The constitution gave the government five years in which to 'demarcate [their lands], protect their possessions and see that they are respected'. When that period ended in 1993, very little had been done.

In the late 1990s, funds from the German government made available under the Group of Seven's Pilot Plan to Protect the Amazon Rainforest, permitted demarcation of many indigenous homelands, including several very large, controversial areas. Yet it is the government itself, at both the federal and local level, which has all too often been the first to flout constitutional rights and turn a blind eye to the invasion of demarcated lands, as the history of the Yanomami shows.

The Onslaught on the Yanomami

Between 1968 and 1978 eleven proposals to delimit Yanomami territory and create an officially protected area were made, among them three from anthropologists Kenneth Taylor and Alcida Ramos. In 1978 the Catholic

Church's Roraima prelacy made a proposal. The idea was inspired by the Xingu Park which had been created in central Brazil as a safe haven for the many tribes displaced by the roads that were pushing through the jungle to connect the new capital, Brasília, with the North and West. All these proposal was ignored by the military regime.

In 1973 the Yanomami had their first prolonged contact with the brutality of the outside world when the army began building a road through their territory. The 1,500 km long road was to provide the missing link in a road network connecting up the Atlantic and Pacific coasts of the South American continent, and to facilitate access to minerals.

No care was taken to vaccinate the construction workers before they came into contact with the indians who lived in the path of the road, or to vaccinate the Indians themselves. Thirteen communities were decimated by influenza, TB and measles before the road was abandoned in 1976.

In 1978 Claudia Andujar, a photographer, horrified by the scenes of suffering she had seen among the Yanomami, joined forces with anthropologist Bruce Albert and lay missionary Carlo Zacquini to found the Campaign for the Creation of the Yanomami Park (CCPY). They wanted an area of nine million hectares traditionally inhabited by the Yanomami to be declared an indigenous reserve.

Meanwhile in 1975 RADAM, the government's aerial survey of the Amazon had revealed large deposits of cassiterite, or tin ore, and uranium and gold inside the Yanomami area. In 1981 gold was discovered at Santa Rosa, in the northeast of Yanomami territory, and hundreds of prospectors moved in. In 1983 Government Decree No. 88985 laid down rules for mining research in indigenous lands, stating that the location of seams in indigenous lands was no justification for the 'non-exploration of mineral resources which are fundamental to national security or to the country's development process'. Thus invasions received official endorsement and FUNAI was powerless to stop them or avoid the devastating consequences for the Indians.

In 1983 congressmen from Roraima began to present the first of many bills proposed over the years with the express purpose of opening up Yanomami lands to mining. Deputies Mozarildo Cavalcanti and João Batista Fagundes had got themselves chosen as members of the Congressional Committee on Indian questions, where they systematically sabotaged attempts to legislate in favour of the Indian population and proposed bills to favour mining and other economic interests. Fagundes tabled a bill permitting the emancipation of Indians, if necessary without their consent. The decision was to be removed from the courts and given to local authorities. Once emancipated, Indians would acquire the rights of individual Brazilian citizens, but they would lose their collective right to their traditional lands. An earlier attempt to introduce compulsory emancipation had been dropped after pro-indigenous groups campaigned vigorously against it.

Also in 1983, Deputy Mozarildo Cavalcanti introduced a bill to allow the opening up of the Surucucus area to cassiterite mining. The bill had the backing of the Roraima state government. This bill became known as the 'genocide' bill. The Surucucus area not only had the biggest concentration of Yanomami, but many villages in the area were still totally isolated. For some, their first contact with outsiders came as incidents between *garimpeiros* and Yanomami multiplied. In support of the bill Deputy Fagundes said 'if we consider that the mineral reserves existed long before the Indian reserves, we will reach the sad conclusion that the Indian reserves were placed on top of these mineral reserves, not to protect Indian rights but to hide the right of Brazil to take possession of its mineral wealth.'

By this time the CCPY had begun a health project in the Yanomami area, and mobile medical teams set about introducing preventive measures. In reply, Deputy Fagundes presented a bill in 1984 banning non-Brazilians from any sort of work in indigenous communities. Many of the missionaries and medical teams were foreigners. As the threat to the Yanomami grew, the CCPY lobbied the government for the creation of the Park. The United Nations joined in with a formal plea for the Park. In 1984 the Yanomami themselves spoke out in a letter to Brazil's first and only indigenous congressman, the Xavante Indian Mario Juruna:

> We Yanomami want you to help us remove the *garimpeiros* from our lands. For two years the *garimpeiros* have been invading Yanomami land, taking our gold, bringing diseases, wanting to take our women, stealing our crops. Last year hundreds of *garimpeiros* began working in the Apiaú river and the Uraricaá river in Roraima, and near the rivers Ia and Cauaburi in Amazonas.
>
> Our lands are not demarcated and we Yanomami want demarcation now, because in two years' time all our land will be invaded by *garimpeiros* and ranchers. We see the ranchers taking the lands of the Macuxi and we do not want this to happen to our lands because we want to live with our women and children in peace. If the *garimpeiros* do not leave our lands we will give one more warning, and if they do not leave then we will fight.

In response to the pressure, the government then declared an area of over seven million hectares as out of bounds.

The two Roraima representatives immediately protested against this alleged attempt to create an 'indigenous nation' within Brazil. Ignoring the Yanomami's own desire for a safe land free of invasion, Deputy Mozarildo attributed the demand for the Park to a 'mysterious commission [the CCPY] presided over by a foreign lady' [Claudia Andujar]. He claimed that their real motive in defending the cause of the Indians was to obtain possession of the natural resources, especially Amazonian minerals: 'Once the Park is created, the Yanomami nation, through their self-proclaimed defenders, will draw up contracts with developed nations to exploit their mineral wealth and promote development'. The Roraima representatives also claimed that in Venezuela there was pressure to set up a similar Park for the Yanomami who lived there, and that this would result in the creation of a large Yanomami country, overlapping the frontier. Mozarildo and Fagundes wanted the 'immense amount of lands which are blocked to any economic activity' to be reduced in size, not protected. Opposing them in Congress were a handful of representatives and senators who defended the proposal for the Park, notably São Paulo senator, Severo Gomes.

But the attack on Yanomami lands was not confined to Brazil. Over the border in Venezuela, a mining company requested 5,000 hectares of Yanomami territory for cassiterite exploration, with the cynical explanation that it would 'contribute to the integration of the Yanomami into national Venezuelan society'.

In 1984 FUNAI redefined the area placed out of bounds to include 149 Yanomami and three Yekuana *malocas*, including the essential space around them needed for hunting, fishing, food growing and and intertribal commu-nication via the hundreds of trails that crisscrossed Yanomami territory. The new proposed area was to be called the Yanomami Indigenous Park, and it was based on a joint study by FUNAI experts and CCPY. Support for the Park came from an unexpected quarter; the SNI, once the dreaded intelli-gence agency of the military regime, was now seeking a new role for itself as the prospect of a return to civilian power drew near. Agents were sent se-cretly to the Yanomami area. As a result of what they saw, the SNI not only decided to back the creation of the Park but also suggested that a new offi-cial organization should be set up to administer it and everything else to do with the Yanomami. It seemed as though the Park would come about. But it still needed to be approved by the Interministerial Group. This group had representatives from all the ministries affected by indigenous issues, but the men who called the shots were those from the Armed Forces. In 1985 FUNAI sent the formal proposal for the Yanomami Park to the Interministerial Group. They shelved it.

In February 1985 *garimpeiro* leader José Altino Machado led 60 armed men on an airborne invasion of the Surucucus base. They quickly cleared a second airstrip. José Altino, an ambitious man, liked to boast about the army of half a million men he had under his command as president of USAGAL, a trade union for Amazon gold miners. The invasion had the support of local politicians and businessmen, and some said their hidden agenda was to destabilize the Roraima government. But the invasion was too blatant and provocative to be ignored by the central government. Federal police were sent in to arrest Altino's men. Another five planeloads of men were intercepted before they could join them.

A month later, in March 1985, the last of the military presidents, General João Batista Figueiredo, handed over power to the civilian vice-president, José Sarney, while Brazil's elected president, Tancredo Neves, lay on his deathbed. President Sarney, who had been a close ally of the military during their 21 years in power, decided to increase the military presence in the 'empty' northern Amazon to protect the frontiers, and in 1986 announced the new project, calling it Calha Norte (Northern Watershed). Its declared aims were to improve infrastructure, attract more settlers and redefine policy towards the region's indigenous reserves. The real purpose of Calha Norte was to reduce Indian lands and facilitate the access of large-scale mining companies rather than *garimpeiros* to the mineral deposits contained in them. But by providing airstrips and roads, it was the *garimpeiros* who most benefited from it.

In the eyes of anthropologist Bruce Albert, the military decided, in spite of the considerable ecological and social costs and the detrimental effect upon the Indian populations, to accept and then control the ragged *garimpeiro* frontier in the Yanomami area, because from their point of view it furthered the fundamental objectives of Calha Norte: the economic and military occupation of the northern Amazon frontier.

In 1988, 150,000 people from all over the world put their signatures to a document addressed to the UN Secretary-General, Javier Pérez de Cuellar, warning that the Yanomami were in danger of extinction. They asked him to demand respect for indigenous people's rights from the Brazilian government. In September that year President Sarney unexpectedly declared that a continuous area of over eight million hectares was to be recognized as in the permanent possession of the Yanomami. His decree was countersigned by General Bayma Denys, chief military adviser and secretary of the National Security Council. Suddenly it seemed as though the tide had turned at last in favour of the Yanomami. But satisfaction at this decision was short-lived. Only two months later, on 18 November 1988, as the international price of gold rose and *garimpeiros* continued to invade the Yanomami area, Sarney repealed his own decree, reducing the Yanomami area by 70 per cent. Instead of a continuous area, the Yanomami were now to be confined to 19 'islands', an archipelago covering less than three million hectares. These 19 separate Yanomami areas were surrounded by areas designated as 'national forest', where mining would be allowed. Three *garimpeiro* reserves were also created inside the Yanomami lands.

The author of this disastrous new division of the Yanomami area was the man who had just become governor of Roraima, Romero Jucá. An economist from the north-east previously chosen to head FUNAI for party political reasons, Jucá had tried to run Indian affairs via satellite images and had been accused of involvement in a shady timber deal on an indigenous reserve. This did not stop him being appointed governor of Roraima, where he became an energetic champion of the cause of the *garimpeiros*, in the bleakest period of Yanomami history.

As the gold rush gathered momentum not only were *garimpeiros* free to roam within the traditional Yanomami area, but the CCPY, the people who could offer medical treatment for the diseases the gold miners brought with them were ordered to leave by FUNAI, the very agency which was supposed to protect the indians. Between 1988 and 1990 the world of the Yanomami was turned upside down. Missionaries, medical missions, anthropologists were banned. *Garimpeiros*, who included among their number wanted criminals and murderers, who brought with them drugs and alcohol, and who took no precautions to avoid spreading malaria and transmitting flu, venereal diseases, and TB to the Indians, were allowed. In one area, Paapiú, where the air force had built an airstrip as part of Calha Norte, ninety percent of the Indians had malaria in 1989. Between 1987 and 1990 it is estimated that 1,500 Yanomami, 15 percent of the Yanomami population in Brazil, died from disease and malnutrition as a direct result of the gold rush.

In October 1989 a federal judge in Brasília accepted the public prosecutor's request for an injunction against the *garimpeiros* who had invaded indigenous territory. The judge ordered the entire Yanomami area to be placed out of bounds to non-Indians and the immediate expulsion of the *garimpeiros*. Both FUNAI and the federal police refused at first to comply, saying they did not have the resources. The *garimpeiros* in their turn appealed to the court, claiming that their human rights had been violated.

Meanwhile the international press had begun to publish pictures of dying Yanomami being carried to hospital. Survival International organized protests outside embassies in Europe and the USA. The American Anthropological Association accused the Brazilian government of complicity in genocide. Senator Severo Gomes organized a senate hearing at which the FUNAI president not only confirmed the terrible reports that were emerging from Roraima, but pleaded for help. The outcry forced the government into action, and the CCPY and other organizations were allowed to return.

In December 1989 the government announced a 90-day operation to evacuate the estimated 45,000 *garimpeiros* who were in the Yanomami area. In January 1990 they set up an emergency medical programme for the Yanomami with the collaboration of non-governmental organizations, including the CCPY. On 9 January, at a surprise meeting in Boa Vista between federal police chief Romeu Tuma and *garimpeiro* leaders, it was announced that the Minister of Justice had approved a proposal by the Roraima government to set up three *garimpeiro* areas at Uraricoera, Uraricoera de Santa Rosa and Catrimani, within the Yanomami area. This was in flagrant violation of the court decision, and of the congressional decision to vote funds for the removal of the *garimpeiros* and for the health operation. Once again, the public outcry forced the proposal to be dropped.

In March 1990 Sarney was succeeded by President Fernando Collor, a youthful, right-wing populist, who set out to change Brazil's image from that of environmental villain to one of green government. He appointed José Lutzenberger, a well-known, controversial ecologist, as his Environment Minister, and started work to get the Earth Summit held in Brazil. The Yanomami situation offered him a unique chance to gain the front pages. Even before he took office, in January 1990 he commanded a well-publicized police operation, codenamed Selva Livre (Free Jungle), to remove the *garimpeiros* and blow up their jungle airstrips.

Destroying the airstrips destroyed the power of the mine owners but did not stop the small-time *garimpeiros* from continuing to prospect. One hundred and ten illegal airstrips were dynamited, but it was not so easy to deal with the rivers, contaminated with the mercury the *garimpeiros* use to separate the alluvial gold from silt and sand. Many villages were abandoned as so many

71

of their inhabitants had died. In April 1991 Collor abolished the 'islands' and introduced a special Yanomami Health District (DSY), dividing their total area into smaller areas under the responsibility of the FNS, FUNAI, and NGOs and religious missions. CCPY, whose share was 35 communities with 1000 people (approximately 10 per cent of the total Yanomami population in Brazil), set up three health posts.

On 15 November 1991, with much pomp and ceremony, President Collor announced his decision to recognize the Yanomami right to a continuous reserve of 9.4 million hectares, approximately 36,000 square miles. Amazon politicians protested vehemently. The previous 12 years had seen 717 mining claims registered by mining companies anxious to exploit not only gold and cassiterite, but silver, tungsten and other minerals believed to lie under Yanomami soil.

Several generals called the decision 'madness'. In Congress, 21 military associations and ex-army commanders from the Amazon demanded the repeal of the reserve and claimed Collor had acted under international pressure. At the 1992 Earth Summit in Rio, the demarcation of the Yanomami reserve counted in Brazil's favour, and gave it credibility for hosting the event. But by the end of the year Collor had been forced to resign to avoid impeachment for corruption. His vice-president Itamar Franco became president, heading a two-year interim government. Sporadic operations to remove *garimpeiros* continued. A geologist reported that they had left behind them in the Yanomami reserve over 600 tons of waste, in the form of broken machinery, pumps, generators, spare parts and even planes, which provided breeding grounds for malarial mosquitoes. To avoid detection, *garimpeiros* took refuge over the frontier in Venezuela. Their presence on the frontier became a constant source of friction. In February 1993 the Venezuelan police arrested 46 of them, and this led to the setting up of a bi-national commission to investigate the frontier problem. A new agreement between FUNAI and the Brazilian Air Force to remove the *garimpeiros* was signed, and Operation Selva Livre recommenced. Within a week more than 2,000 were said to have left voluntarily while another 40 were forcibly removed by police. In July federal police reported that about 4,000 *garimpeiros* had been removed and 500 grammes of gold had been confiscated. In Congress efforts to reduce the size of the Yanomami reserve continued. The next month news of the Haximú massacre emerged.

A congressional report set out new policies in an attempt to exert more control over informal-sector goldmining in the Amazon region. In 1994

SIVAM, a billion-dollar project to provide a satellite communications system to cover the Amazon region, was announced. The complex information and telecommunications programme was designed to provide radar control and monitoring of all flights, including the hundreds of clandestine drug dealers' and gold miners' planes. The system will allegedly be able to monitor forest fires and river pollution and detect invasions of Indian reserves and illegal goldmining and airstrips.

In December 1995, eight years after first requesting permission from the Brazilian government to visit the Yanomami and investigate accusations of human rights violations, the Human Rights commission of the OAS was allowed to make the visit. They later reported finding that state actions in Roraima had contributed to a deterioration in indigenous peoples' human rights. They also found that the protection offered to the Yanomami by the state against invading *garimpeiros* and the environmental pollution they caused was 'irregular and weak, maintaining a permanent situation of danger and a continuing deterioration of their habitat'.

In January 1995 Itamar Franco was succeeded by President Fernando Henrique Cardoso, who introduced controversial Decree No. 1775, which allowed interested parties to contest the demarcation of many indigenous areas. Although the Yanomami reserve was officially safe, the decree was interpreted as a green light for the invasion of indigenous lands in general. In January 1996, 280 Yanomami leaders from 27 villages held a four-day assembly to discuss their situation, and produced a letter addressed to 'The White Chiefs', namely President Cardoso, Justice Minister Nelson Jobim, Attorney-General Geraldo Brandão and the head of FUNAI, Marcos Santilli. It said:

> We don't want *garimpeiros* on our land because they are very bad, they pollute our rivers and creeks, they make holes in the ground looking for gold the fish die, the game die. All the Yanomami are dying because the *garimpeiros* bring diseases that kill us: malaria and influenza. For this reason we don't want *garimpeiros* or other whites: ranchers, politicians, loggers, soldiers, fishermen. We don't want a small territory. We want a large area, the way it was demarcated. Don't reduce the size of our land. We want to keep this large, unbroken area.

In spite of the Yanomami appeal, in March 1996 funds ran out for FUNAI's operation to maintain permanent surveillance of the Yanomami area, and it was suspended. Within 24 hours, planes were sighted flying in prospectors and machinery, and soon *garimpeiros* were reported to be distributing guns to

Yanomami. Several cases of death and injury from gunshot wounds were reported. In London later the same month Justice Minister Nelson Jobim promised an immediate operation to remove the *garimpeiros* who had re-invaded the Yanomami area. Nothing happened. The same year the Brazilian Catholic church's missionary organization, CIMI, published a report saying that in 1994/95, one third (106,000) of the indigenous population was suffering from malnutrition, a dramatic rise on the previous figures. They reported the murder of 75 Indians, and the attempted murder of 276 in the same period. Forty-six reserves, mostly in the Amazon region, had suffered new invasions, which CIMI blamed on Government Decree 1775.

In November 1997, 18 months after it had been suspended, and following repeated lobbying by the CCPY, Survival International and many other Brazilian and overseas organizations, the removal operation began again, and lasted for three months. This time it was a joint operation involving the Justice Ministry, the Federal Police, the Public Prosecutor's Office and the armed forces. Nearly 2,000 *garimpeiros* were removed. At the same time, President Cardoso announced a new defence policy, saying that the Amazon region had replaced Argentina and the southern frontiers as Brazil's priority concern. He proposed increasing the military presence on Amazon frontiers and turning them into 'living' frontiers, meaning colonization. For Cardoso, the new threat to Brazil's Amazon region comes from drug cartels and guerrilla bands in neighbouring countries. In 1997 President Cardoso authorized funding for the paving of the BR 174 road between Manaus and Boa Vista (the road between Boa Vista and the Venezuelan border was already paved). Thus there is now a 1600-km road connecting Manaus in the heart of the Amazon to Caracas on the Caribbean, bringing the Northern Hemisphere much nearer for Brazilian exports, but also facilitating the arrival in Roraima of those in search of land, gold and fortune.

Brazil and Venezuela also agreed in 1997 to build a 685-km overhead power line to bring electricity from the Guri dam on the Caroni River in Venezuela to Roraima's capital, Boa Vista. Although this took the pressure off building a dam inside Makuxi land in Roraima, the line passes through other indigenous areas in Brazil and Venezuela, and through a national park and UN World Heritage site, Canaima, in Venezuela. The two governments have plans for many other giant development projects in the region, including more highways, oil and gas pipelines and industrial waterways. With Guyana, the Brazilian government has plans to improve the road between Georgetown and Boa Vista. In August 1997 these projects and many others planned for the region by the three governments, were discussed at the first ever seminar of indigenous leaders from the three countries.

In a statement the 80 leaders said they represented 35,000 Indians who lived in the savannah and forests of the three-country frontier region, which contained the headwaters of the three great South American river basins – the Amazon, the Orinoco and the Essequibo. They criticized the way in which the rights, views and participation of the indigenous populations, on whose way of life the proposed infrastructure projects would have a huge impact, had been completely ignored. They demanded that 'our territories should no longer be considered "empty spaces", to be occupied and exploited', but should all be demarcated, and kept free of intruders and other forms of occupation and pressure. No more military bases should be built in indigenous territories. Indians living in frontier areas should be allowed to come and go freely. They should decide about the use of renewable and non-renewable resources in their own lands. They wanted governments to support indigenous people's own projects for education, health, radio communications networks, transport and economic activities. International funding for the infrastructure projects should be released only when these demands had been met, said the gathered leaders.

In December 1997 President Cardoso launched a national programme on human rights, saying 'my government is committed to the promotion of human rights'. Among the 'short-term actions' listed for the indigenous population it proposed to 'ensure that representatives of the indigenous population and organizations take an active part in decisions and policy-making regarding the protection and promotion of indigenous rights.' Shortly after, the government opened a site on the Internet welcoming investment in Roraima and extolling its attractions: millions of acres of fertile land, roads and infrastructure. There was no mention of the fact that 24 per cent of the state's population belongs to indigenous communities, occupying 43 per cent of the state's area, or any suggestion that consultation with them might be necessary.

THE BRAZILIAN GOVERNMENT'S HUMAN RIGHTS PROGRAMME FOR INDIGENOUS PEOPLE

Short-term actions

• Devise and implement policies to protect and promote the rights of the Indigenous Population, and abandon paternalistic attitudes and assimilation policies.
• Support the reform of the Indian Statute (Act no. 6001/73), so as to incorporate the changes proposed in the bill on the Statute of the Indigenous Population, already approved by the Chamber of Deputies.
• Ensure that representatives of the Indigenous population and organizations take active part in decisions and policy-making regarding the protection and promotion of indigenous rights.
• Guarantee the rights of the indigenous population to the lands they traditionally occupy.
• Demarcate and legally recognize all the lands traditionally occupied by the indigenous population.
• Contribute to efforts to increase mutual trust between governmental and non-governmental organizations, through seminars, workshops and projects that combat misinformation and fear, which may lead to conflicts and violence against the indigenous population.
• Provide the National Indian Foundation — FUNAI — with the necessary material resources for the performance of its task of protecting the rights of the indigenous population, especially regarding land demarcation.
• Ensure health care to the indigenous population, taking into account their specific needs and characteristics.
• Ensure schooling and education to the indigenous population, respecting their specific social and cultural background.
• Promote public awareness and knowledge, through the media and the school system, about the indigenous population and their rights, since misinformation is one of the root causes of discrimination and violence against them.

Medium-term actions

• Create a system of permanent survey over Indian lands, in order to protect them against intruders, using mobile inspection units and trained personnel recruited among members of the Indian community.
• Collect information on conflicts involving Indian lands, and include it in the map of land conflicts and rural violence in Brazil.

Long-term actions

• Restructure FUNAI in order to enable it to perform the task of protecting the rights of the indigenous population more effectively.
• Support the development of economically, environmentally and culturally sustainable projects by indigenous communities.

THE HEALTH OF THE YANOMAMI

Malaria: 1997 (12 months) 4,289 cases
1998 (first 6 months) 4,152 = increase of 93.6 per cent.

Infant Mortality: 1991-97 annual rate = 134.2
1998 first half = 197.4 = increase of 47.1 per cent.

TB: 1991–97 annual Yanomami rate: 584 (12 times higher than non-Yanomami rate; annual Brazilian rate: 50).

Death: 1991-97 Annual mortality rate: 1,440
1991–97 annual mortality rate for Brazilian population: 600

Cause of death: 1991–June 1998: 1,211 Yanomami died.
Three main causes: Cause unknown: 35.1 per cent
Malaria: 23.4 per cent
Acute respiratory infections: 13.2 per cent

Health care is divided between the government agency, FNS, responsible for 13 areas, and six non-governmental organizations, responsible for 11 areas, coordinated by the FNS under the name Yanomami Health District (DSY). On the whole the health indicators are much better in those areas attended by NGOs.

Source: WHO, 1998

In March 1998 the world was once more alarmed by news that the Yanomami were in danger, this time from fire. A prolonged drought, worsened by the effects of El Niño weather phenomenon, had left the trees tinder dry, so that when Roraima farmers began to clear their land with the traditional slash and burn techniques, the fires spread out of control. The worst-hit areas were in the savannah, home to 20,000 Makuxi and Wapixana Indians, but it was the potential threat to the rainforest home of the Yanomami that brought the international press rushing once more to Roraima. Once the fires had become headline news in the world's press, the federal government, which had ignored pleas for help from the Roraima authorities for two months, finally acted. Hundreds of firefighters were called up from all over Brazil, and a special task force came from Argentina to help the underequipped local firemen to fight the fires, which spread over hundreds of miles. But it was the providential arrival of rain that finally put out the fires, just as they began to lick the edges of the Yanomami reserve. Only a small part of the Yanomami area was burnt, but the drought blighted crops and brought hunger. The smoke from the fires also prevented medical teams flying into the area and the number of malaria cases increased.

At the end of 1998 the Yanomami's health situation had declined dramatically, due to the drastic cuts imposed on FUNAI and the FNS as part of the government's austerity measures, aided and abetted by corruption and incompetence at the local level. Attempts continued in Congress to open up indigenous areas to mining and to reduce the size of the Yanomami area.

Unwittingly and often reluctantly, the Yanomami have played an important role in both Brazilian politics and in the wider world's perception of the indigenous peoples of the Americas. No other indigenous people in Brazil has provoked so much legislation. And no other people has cost the Brazilian government's reputation so dear over the decades: Brazil has been denounced to the United Nations and the Organization of American States for genocide and cast in the role of villain in international forums because of its treatment of the Yanomami. The gold rush and its sponsors, the military and civilian governments, brought huge social and environmental costs to both the indigenous and white populations of Roraima, but economically very few benefited. Most of the gold left Brazil without being taxed, while the cost of repairing the environmental damage and of providing health-care has been left to the state and the NGOs.

Few indigenous groups have captured the imagination of the world quite so powerfully as the Yanomami. There is perhaps a feeling that because of their direct link with the world of the rainforest, because they are themselves a link with the past, they must not be destroyed.

APPENDIX

Radio message from FUNAI in a Yanomami area to FUNAI HQ in Brasília, advising that gold miners were threatening Indians with firearms.
9th August 1993

Message from FUNAI office in Boa Vista to FUNAI HQ in Brasília with news of the murder of five or six Yanomami youths and an increase in gold miners' activities. 10th August 1993

Letter from FUNAI HQ in Brasília to Federal Police in Boa Vista requesting inquiry into newspaper report of new gold miner invasion of Yanomami area being planned. 12th August 1993

Fundação Nacional do Índio
MINISTÉRIO DA JUSTIÇA

OFÍCIO Nº 04/ /PG/93   Brasília, 12 de agosto de 1993

Senhor Diretor,

Cumpre-me encaminhar a V.Sª, para conhecimento e adoção das providências necessárias, cópia de uma reportagem publicada no Jornal "Zero Hora", edição de 27.07.93, sob o título "Os garimpeiros tramam a volta à Área Yanomami".

De acordo com a citada matéria, grupos organizados de garimpeiros, incentivados por autoridades locais, estariam ultimando preparativos para burlar a vigilância da FUNAI e invadir, novamente, as terras pertencentes aos índios Yanomami.

Isto posto, solicito a V.Sª determinar a instauração do competente inquérito policial para apurar as denúncias constantes da citada publicação, além de reforçar a vigilância da Área Indígena Yanomami, evitando, com isso, que novas invasões daquela área venham a ocorrer.

Atenciosamente,

Marcelo Luiz C. Rodoplano de Oliveira
Proc. Geral Subst. FUNAI

ILMO SR.
Diretor do Departamento de Polícia Federal em Roraima
Boa Vista - RR

PG/GWFS.ibs

Radio message from FUNAI in Surucucus advising of discovery of human skeletons and other signs of a massacre. 19th August 1993

```
                                              205 P01      AUG 19 '93  13:35

                                        ┌─────────────────┐
                                        │ ADM. REG.  RR   │
                                        │ SETEL . FUNAI   │
                                        │ Em 19/08/93     │
                                        └─────────────────┘

FUNDAÇÃO NACIONAL DO INDIO          ADR BOA VISTA.
RADIOTELEGRAMA RECEBIDO

DE  SURUCUCUNR      20 PLS 60      DT  19/08 HS 1645   FR

RECEBIDO DE  SRO    1908    ÀS   1745    POR  FR/FCO

ADM REG ADM BVB/POI FEDERAL/BVB                    CONTROLE
```

499/SRB DT 190893 PT INFO QUE EQUIPE PCI FEDERAL ET FUNAI SOBREVOANDO
AREAA EM HELICOPTERO LOCALIZOU AS DUAS MALOCAS HOXIMU TOTALMENTE DES-
TRUIDA VIRTUDE INCENDIO VG ENCONTRANDO NO LOCAL UTENSILIOS COMO PA-
NELAS FLAXEAS AR TIROS ET CORIADAS DE FACAO VG INDIOS INDICARAM LO
CAL PARA ONDE SOBREVIVENTES FUGIRAM APOS ATAQUE VG NA MATA FOCALIZA-
DOS DIVERSOS TAPIRIS ONDE SOBREVIVENTES ESCONDERAM ET LOCAL DE NO-
VO ATAQUE SENDO RECOLHIDO DIVERSOS CARTUCHOS DE ARMAS DE CAÇA VG SEN-
DO ENCONTRADOS TAMBEM ESQUELETOS HUMANOS EM ADIANTADO ESTADO DE FUTRI
FICAO VG INDIOS INFORMARAM QUE CORPOS FORAM CARREGADOS POR PARENTES
E NA MALOCA DE SIMAO ONDE REALIZOU-SE STRIMORIA DE CARMAÇÃO BOSFOGA-
POS VG RELATARAM AO DOS SOBREVIVENTE S AFOSTANDO FOR DIVERSOS SEG-
MENTOS QUE RESTARAM DE UMA DAS MALOCAS ESTIMA SE QUE ESTAVA NO LOCAL
EM MOMENTO DE 30 PESSOAS PELO MENOS NA MALOCA DOS SOBREVIVENTES QUE
SERVIU DE GUIA INCLUSIVE ENTREVISTANE PERDEU O PAI ET OS DOIS IRMAOS
NAO POSSUIA MAE POR TER SIDO VITIMA DE MALARIA A TEMPOS ATRAS PT
DELEGADO POI FEDERAL/WILK CELIO

ASSINATURA

ACRONYMS

CCPY   *Commissão pro-Yanomami*
            Pro-Yanomami Commission

CEDI   *Centro Ecuménico de Documentação e Informação*
            Ecumencial Centre for Documentation and Information

CIMI   *Conselho Indigenista Missionario*
            Indian Missionary Council

CIR   *Conselho Indigena de Roraima*
            Indigenous Council of Roraima

CODESAIMA   *Companhía de Desenvolvimento de Roraima*
            Roraima Development Council

DNPM   *Departamento Nacional de Produção Mineral*
            National Department for Mineral Production

DSY   *Distrito de Saúde Yanomami*
            Yanomami Health District

FUNAI   *Fundação Nacional do Indio*
            National Indian Foundation

FNS   *Fundação Nacional da Saúde*
            National Health Foundation

IBAMA   *Instituto Brasileiro de Meio Ambiente e Recursos Renováveis*
            Brazilian Institute for the Environment and Natural Resources

INCRA   *Instituto Nacional de Colonização e Reforma Agraria*
            National Institute for Colonization and Land Reform

MEVA   *Missão Evangélica da Amazônia*
            Amazon Evangelical Mission

MMA   *Ministerio do Meio Ambiente e Amazônia Legal*
            Ministry of the Environment and the Amazon Region

OAS   *Organização dos Estados Americanos*
            Organization of American States (OAS)

SPI   *Serviço de Proteção aos Indios*
            Indian Protection Service

USAGAL   *União de Sindicatos dos Garimpeiros de Amazônia Legal*
            Union of Amazonian Goldminers

82

GLOSSARY

Brazilian Indigenous Terms

beijú	flat pancake made from manioc flour
cutía	small animal
genipapo	plant dye
igarapé	stream
ingá	fruit
maloca	communal house or village
tapiri	temporary shelter
-theri	inhabitant/s
timbó	vine used for fish poison
tuxaua	chief

Portuguese Terms

balsa	raft, dredge used for mining alluvial
barração	shed, trading post
cabaça	gourd
caboclo	mixed blood or pure Indian living like a white man, making a living from agriculture or fishing
garimpeiro	prospector or miner
garimpo	mining camp, claim
pista	runway, airstrip
posseiro	small farmer without formal title to his land: he can acquire land rights after five years living and working on it
roça	plot of land for growing food, vegetable garden
terco/facão	long knife

BIBLIOGRAPHY

ACAO PELA CIDADANIA: Yanomami: A Todos os Povos da Terra: São Paulo
CCPY/CEDI/CIMI/NDI 1990

ALBERT, BRUCE:Terra indígena, politica ambiental e geopolítica do desenvolvimento da
Amazonia no Brasil: o caso Yanomami: Urihi No 8

ALBERT, BRUCE: Desenvolvimento militar e garimpo no norte amazónico: os índios
Yanomami face ao Projeto Calha Norte. Antropologia e Indigenismo. Rio de Janeiro:
Museu Nacional

ALBERT, BRUCE: O massacre dos Yanomami de Haximú: Povos Indígenas no Brasil, 1991-
1995, pp. 203-207: São Paulo: Instituto Socioambiental 1996

AMNESTY INTERNATIONAL: "We are the land" indigenous peoples' struggle for human
rights: London 1992

CEJIL (Centro pela Justiça e o Direito Internacional) : Petitions to Interamerican
Commission on Human Rights of the Organization of American States, accusing
Brazilian and Venezuelan governments of responsibility, through negligence and
omission, for the Haximú massacre: Washington: 1996

CIMI/CNBB: A Violencia contra os Povos Indígenas no Brasil 1996: Brasília 1997

COLCHESTER, MARCUS: Sustentabilidad y toma de decisiones en el Amazonas
venezolano: Los yanomamis en la reserva de la Biósfera del Alto Orinoco-Casiquiare:
from the book Amazonas Modernidad en Tradición. Sada Amazonas GTZ: Caracas
1995

MacMILLAN, GORDON: At the End of the Rainbow? Gold, Land and People in the
Brazilian Amazon: Earthscan 1995

MAGALHAES, EDGARD DIAS and CAVALCANTI, LUCIANO GOMES, Morbi-
Mortalidade Yanomami - 1991 a 1997: UFRR 1998

RAMOS, ALCIDA RITA: A Profecia de um boato, matando por ouro na área Yanomami:
Anuario Antropológico: Rio de Janeiro: Tempo Brasileiro, 1996

RAMOS, ALCIDA RITA: Yanomami: A Homeland Undermined : updated translation of
the Expert Report written at the request of the Attorney General's Office, Brasília 1989

RAMOS, ALCIDA RITA: Reflecting on the Yanomami: Ethnographic Images and the
Pursuit of the Exotic: Cultural Anthropology 1987

RAMOS, ALCIDA RITA: Yanoama Indians in Northern Brazil threatened by highway:
from Yanoama in Brazil, edited by Alcida R.Ramos and Kenneth Taylor, International
Work Group for Indigenous Affairs document 37, pp 1-41 : Copenhagen 1979

SPONSEL, LESLIE E: The Master Thief: Gold Mining and Mercury Contamination in the
Amazon: London 1997

SURVIVAL: 'When the Sky Fell', Newsletter No 27: London 1990

SURVIVAL: YANOMAMI : A Story of Genocide: London 1990

UPDATES: newsletters of the CCPY 1984-98

WAGNER, CARLOS: Zero Hora: Porto Alegre 27/3/93

Survival International

Survival International is the only organization of its kind. Started in Britain in 1969 in response to massacres of indigenous peoples in Amazonia, Survival now has supporters in over 80 countries and works for tribal peoples' rights through campaigns, education and funding. We work closely with local indigenous organizations and focus on tribal peoples who have the most to lose, often those most recently in contact with the outside world.

We set out to demolish the myth that tribal peoples are relics, destined to perish through 'progress'. We promote respect for their cultures and explain the contemporary relevance of their way of life. We also produce material for children, the conscience of the future. We enable tribes to talk directly to companies invading their land. We point out the threats, giving them the information they need to make their voices heard.

Survival is the only organization of its kind which refuses money from governments – ensuring our freedom of action and making us stretch our resources to the limit.

Since 1969, the world's attitude to tribal peoples has changed. Then, it was assumed that they would die out or be assimilated, now, at least in some places, their experience and values are considered important. Survival has pushed tribal issues into the mainstream. This, perhaps, is our greatest achievement, but there are many barriers of racism, tyranny and greed still to overcome.

Tribal peoples need your help. Please write or phone for more information and membership details.

Survival International
11-15 Emerald Street
London WC1N 3QL
Tel: 0171 242 1441
Fax: 0171 242 1441
email: survival@gn.apc.org
Website: www.survival.org.uk

CCPY

The Pro Yanomami Commission (CCPY) is a Brazilian non-governmental organization which has worked with the Yanomami in the defence of their land and culture since 1979. It runs health and educational projects with a number of Yanomami communities. It provides continuous health care to approximately 1,000 Yanomami living in 20 communities, and is developing an integrated education programme in order to assist the Yanomami in their evolving contact with the technological world, as well as enabling them to develop economic alternatives whilst simultaneously preserving their culture and natural resources. They are currently setting up an agro-forestry project.

For futher information please contact:

CCPY - Comissão Pró Yanomami
Rua Manoel da Nobrega 111 - cj. 32
04.001-900
São Paulo
SP
Brazil

Tel: +55 11 289 1200
Fax: +55 11 284 6997
email: ccpysp@uol.com.br

Survival's and CCPY's Yanomami Campaign

In November 1991, President Collor signed a decree creating an Indian 'Park' covering all Yanomami lands in Brazil. This was the result of many years of vigorous campaigning by the Pro Yanomami Commission (CCPY) in Brazil and Survival worldwide – a campaign which was supported in the end by tens of thousands of people and many organizations.

The campaign started twenty years before with Survival president Robin Hanbury-Tenison's mission to investigate atrocities against Brazilian Indians. He supported the proposal for a Yanomami Park already drawn up by anthropologists Kenneth I. Taylor and Alcida Ramos.

Over the next few years several support groups were formed in Brazil, and in 1978 Claudia Andujar founded the CCPY. The Yanomami were threatened by a new road and by moves to split their land into separate 'pockets'. Thirteen communities were decimated – some were virtually wiped out. Once again a Park project, co-authored by anthropologist Bruce Albert, was proposed. The government started making promises about Yanomami land – promises which were to be consistently and repeatedly broken for the next 13 years.

The campaign continued unabated through the 1980s, to be stepped up in 1989 when the 10,000 Yanomami were invaded by 40,000 illegal gold prospectors. This new and overwhelming onslaught marked a turning point. The number of Indian deaths rocketed – no less than 1,500 Yanomami were killed by disease and violent confrontation with the miners.

Although the Yanomami have their land recognised, this does not guarantee their survival. It only gives the Yanomami the right to use the area. Mineral rights remain with the state and there are at least 20 mining companies who want to get in. As well as this, the army can enter and use the frontier zone as it wishes. Unlike other Amazonian countries, in Brazil no Indians actually own their land; they have the right only to use it – an important difference (and one which violates international law). And although nothing less than another Presidential decree can cancel the Park in the future, Indian lands have been revoked in this way before.

In the last few years, gold miners have reinvaded the area, and malaria and other diseases are still prevalent in some regions. It is still essential that the CCPY and other health teams continue to work in the area.

The struggle for Yanomami survival is far from over. But there is no doubt that without the Park the Indians would have been doomed to eventual, probably quite rapid, annihilation and that now their chances of living into the 21st century are higher that they have been for a generation.

The thirty year Survival and CCPY action proves that a sharply focussed public campaign, properly coordinated, unrelenting, and with a consistent long-term view and thoughtful strategy, can bring major changes for the better in the way tribal peoples are treated. In many situations, nothing else will work.

LAB Books

The Brazil Reader (eds Robert Levine and John J Crocitti) 1999 £16.99
A new anthology which brings a fresh perspective to the traditional disciplines of history, politics, and economics and new approaches to understanding social life - gender, the history of the family, and collective memory.

Benedita da Silva (as told to Medea Benjamin & Maisa Mendonça) 1998 £12.99
The inspiring story of a truly remarkable woman, who fought poverty, racism and exclusion to become Brazil's first black woman senator.

Brazil in Focus (Jan Rocha) 1997 £5.99
A pocket-sized introduction to the country, with sections on history, the economy, society and culture, plus 'where to go, what to see' advice for visitors.

Faces of Latin America (Duncan Green) updated edition 1997 £10.99
'A journalistic tour de force with academic worth ... recommended as essential background reading for many an undergraduate course in the Latin American studies area.' Bulletin of Hispanic Studies.

Return of the Indian (Phillip Wearne) 1996 £14.99
'A great book, educational and informative. It's a must read for those who are interested in indigenous peoples' issues.' Matthew Coon Come, Grand Chief, Grand Council of the Crees of Quebec.

Green Guerrillas (ed. Helen Collinson) 1996 £10.99
Profiles the people on the frontline of an environmental war, from indigenous groups and forest settlers, to fishing communities, peasant farmers, flower workers, shanty-town activists and many more.

Women in Brazil (Caipora Womens' Group) 1993 £5.99
A mosaic of articles, poems and interviews giving an evocative picture of life for women in Brazil's shanty towns and peasant villages.

You can order these books directly from:
Latin America Bureau, FREEPOST KE7728, London EC1B 1TW. No stamp required if posted in the UK.
Please add 10% for post and packing.